GESTALT
COUNSELLING
in a nutshell

SAGE has been part of the global academic community since 1965, supporting high quality research and learning that transforms society and our understanding of individuals, groups and cultures. SAGE is the independent, innovative, natural home for authors, editors and societies who share our commitment and passion for the social sciences.

Find out more at: **www.sagepublications.com**

Gaie Houston

GESTALT
COUNSELLING
in a nutshell

⑤SAGE

Los Angeles | London | New Delhi
Singapore | Washington DC

COUNSELLING IN A NUTSHELL SERIES: Edited by Windy Dryden

Los Angeles | London | New Delhi
Singapore | Washington DC

SAGE Publications Ltd
1 Oliver's Yard
55 City Road
London EC1Y 1SP

SAGE Publications Inc.
2455 Teller Road
Thousand Oaks, California 91320

SAGE Publications India Pvt Ltd
B 1/I 1 Mohan Cooperative Industrial Area
Mathura Road
New Delhi 110 044

SAGE Publications Asia-Pacific Pte Ltd
3 Church Street
#10-04 Samsung Hub
Singapore 049483

Editor: Alice Oven
Editorial assistant: Kate Wharton
Production editor: Rachel Burrows
Copyeditor: Fern Bryant
Proofreader: Jill Birch
Marketing manager: Tamara Navaratnam
Cover design: Wendy Scott
Typeset by: C&M Digitals (P) Ltd, Chennai, India
Printed by: Replika Press Pvt Ltd, India

Library of Congress Control Number: 2012930920

British Library Cataloguing in Publication data

A catalogue record for this book is available from
the British Library

ISBN 978-1-4462-0837-3
ISBN 978-1-4462-0838-0 (pbk)

This book is gratefully dedicated to all the supervisees who over the years have shared their knowledge and experience with me, and given me much of the material for the highly edited case vignettes throughout this book.

Contents

About the Author

Gaie Houston Dip. A.B.Sc., has a degree in English literature from Oxford University, and had her first training in gestalt in the United States. She has taught and practised gestalt therapy and organisational behaviour in London since the 1970s, and currently in many places outside the UK. She has written 18 radio plays broadcast by the BBC, and more recently has directed operas in this country and Italy. She has written a number of books on gestalt, group behaviour, supervision and integrative therapy. She is currently Emeritus Adviser to The Gestalt Centre, London, and on the editorial board of three gestalt journals. She sees global warming as the most urgent issue for everyone now.

Foreword

This book sets out to be an account of gestalt therapy theory and practice. Over the years and in different cultures, there has inevitably been Darwinian change and development in both these areas. Though emphases have changed in different trainings and countries, a core of assumptions and methods persist. These I hope to describe here, with reference to a number of the many other variations that are current. In this short account I have quoted few writers, and of necessity left out the names of many of the worldwide contributors to the evolution of this still under-researched but undeniably effective form of psychotherapy.

As quoted more than once in the following chapters, Laura Perls, one of the co-founders of gestalt therapy, said that every new patient requires a new therapy. The best I would hope from your reading this is that you feel well informed about this optimistic and co-operative form of psychotherapy. If you are a practitioner, I hope you will be empowered to respond, within a clear theoretical discipline, yet freely and creatively, to your clients, and so create another new therapy. In this way gestalt can continue to encourage excitement and growth, and what the Buddhists term 'right living', in all parties to it.

ONE

Human Nature and Gestalt

Note: *There will be many references in this book to what is properly called gestalt therapy theory. As this phrase is cumbersome, I will generally shorten it to just the word gestalt.*

'When will you, at last, become that which you truly are?' Maria Theresa of Austria [in a letter to her daughter Marie Antoinette twenty years before the guillotine came down].

Most of us have some notion of that which we truly are. Plato saw this as an aspiration, an ideal that could never be fulfilled, but which showed a direction to aspire to. Somewhere in every counsellor, whether it is overt or not, is a belief about what we call human nature. In fact it is rare indeed for anyone to be without various convictions about what we are really like, or what makes us tick. It is one which has to be the starting place for all therapy, the more because different people have different assumptions about what makes us behave as we do. So we can begin by reminding ourselves, by raising our awareness, of some of these different beliefs, all immensely powerful in how they shape people's behaviour.

Fritz Perls, influenced by his wife Laura, and the first writer about gestalt therapy, said, 'Man seems to be born with a sense of social and psychological balance as acute as his sense of physical balance' (1978: 27). He was a psychoanalyst whose first book, *Ego, Hunger and Aggression*, was subtitled *A Revision of Freud's Theories* (1969[1947]). This revision was in some instances a rebellion; in other parts it supported some of Freud's method and insights. And he searched for an improvement to the theories already there, even calling gestalt 'the psychology of the obvious'.

And he embraced ideas from many sources in Eastern and Western thinking, taking them further, into his powerful and optimistic view of human nature. Rather than offer the gestalt therapy view straightaway, we can look very briefly at some of the many others.

Religions can seem the authorities on the subject, and all religions that I have heard of provide their own answers to this question. For Buddhists we are creatures condemned to recurrent life on this earth, in various forms, depending on how virtuously we live each of these lives, until we achieve the highest good. Christianity contains a story of self-sacrifice for the general good, and a list of socially useful prohibitions, intended to promote acceptable behaviour. As in many religions, these advocate social awareness and responsibility. They have needed to do this, supposedly, because they originated in times and places where there was plenty of the opposite.

Psychology is a formalisation of this study of what we do and what makes us do it. It is a study with which humans have no doubt been busy since they could first string concepts together, and which most of us embroider, as we try to account for our own or other people's behaviour. Unlike many religions, professional psychologists study behaviour and motivation as it occurs, rather than saying what everyone ought to be doing. They look at what does happen or seems to happen, rather than what ought to happen.

We are all psychologists. We all study behaviour and have our personal theories of human nature. He's trying to wind you up. She doesn't know what she's doing. You can't trust women. You can think of dozens of confident statements like this. Philosophers from ancient times have written theories of human nature, often with some prompts about how to be good, virtuous, the right kind of person. They evidently felt the urge to add morality to psychology. In ancient Greece there was a long study of virtue, and the virtuous man. Women were not always an important part of this ethos. Neither were slaves. On the other hand, homosexuality and pederasty were accepted, and heterosexuality sometimes seen as a necessary evil. Here is just one example of how human nature is quite differently construed at different times and in different places. Truth, rather than being the universal archly stated by Jane Austen, is contextual, only valid according to circumstances.

Anthropologists and many others puzzle still over whether there is universal human nature, shared by everyone, as they notice all that is culturally bound, belonging just to particular groups. In this important search for understanding us, Plato (Meno: 77e) suggested that nobody knowingly wants anything bad. This statement has been contested by many later thinkers and observers. But he went on to conclude that it is lack of knowledge that leads to bad behaviour. This powerful belief underlies gestalt therapy. The raising of awareness, which is the access to knowledge, is made the task, the cornerstone of this new therapy.

Awareness and the unconscious

When Plato spoke of knowledge, it looks as if he was thinking of what is or can be in awareness. This means, to a great extent, knowing about things like riding a bike, how to eat artichokes, or build a nuclear reactor. Nobody is born knowing how to do these things. A good deal of rationality is needed in order to learn them.

There is on the other hand a great deal that we do without seeming to learn, like digesting food, pumping blood, mending wounds, finding what work we really want, or where we know we want to live, and with whom. Even before birth, the human embryo seems to grow through the stages of evolution of the whole species. In other words, somewhere in us there is this vast memory, the working knowledge of how to become a human at the first stages of development. We know how to evolve from a few-cell organism stage, through the reptilian, and on, so that we emerge into the world as one of a very sophisticated, a highly evolved, species. It is common, and understandable, to call these growth processes, and many of the maintenance processes we carry on throughout life, unconscious. We tend not to notice them, at least if they are functioning well. But here we are, and so here is the proof that we know how to become and remain our changing selves.

Perls challenged the common use of the words unconscious mind. It is indeed an odd concept, defining something by what it is not. He laid great emphasis on the raising of awareness. But a confusion of language and meaning can follow from that.

The words conscious and aware are generally used interchangeably. Yet the word conscious has a root meaning that does not have to imply awareness. It means 'with knowledge'. Describing what are sometimes called vegetative processes, of digestion and growth and so on, it is clear that there has to be a species of knowledge, indeed highly detailed knowledge, to enable such things to happen. I have to know what foods disagree with me and need to be expelled fast. I have to keep a most exact watch on body temperature. And so forth. Some of this knowledge seems inherited, and some I clearly learn along the way, for instance in adaptations of the immune system as more hazards are successfully met through life. As I write I marvel at the extraordinary range and complexity of all this knowledge that Perls included in the term the wisdom of the organism.

This term acknowledges how worthy of respect are the infinity of contributions to our health, to our lives, that happen outside awareness. What a noble piece of work is man. In the chapter on theory there is more about awareness. What is written here first is by way of introduction to an aspect of the gestalt understanding of human nature.

Sigmund Freud came to his revolutionary ideas about human nature at a time when in much of the Christian world people believed firmly in original sin, in babies being born bad, and needing to be forced into goodness. It was a time when sex was a taboo subject of discussion, if rather the reverse in practice. In this context, he conceived the idea that two forces struggle within us, one towards destruction and death, the other towards love, creativity and life. He also decided that the aetiology, the origins, of all neurosis was to do with the sexual drive. These are large statements about our nature.

Fritz Perls, a Freudian analyst of a rebellious kind, grew restive in this belief system. He believed that the flow of life is at best between the excitement of new experience and growth, and achieving homeostasis, the return to balance, a temporary peace, after attending to a need. He insisted on the integrity, the oneness, of all that we have divided by language into mind, spirit and body, and importantly the environment, the context in which we are from moment to moment.

Perls said explicitly that mental activity seems to be activity of the whole person, carried on at a lower energy level than those activities we call physical (1978: 14). Hard evidence on this observation has now come from neuroscience, as we have been able to scan how thinking and imagining bring about vestiges of the same body behaviour that would be there in fully enacting whatever is going on in the mind. Though convention says otherwise, it is easy to understand that mind and body are indivisible. If there is no body, there is no mind. Mind can be defined as the hugely varied, almost magical functions of the brain. Once the brain is dead, so is the person. What may be harder to grasp, in such an individualistic society as exists in many parts of the world now, is that without the world, there is no I or you. At planet level, yes, that is obvious. But gestalt insists on our being indivisible from our surroundings. That is an idea that seems to challenge Western notions of independence. I am free. I decide. Yes, perhaps. But gestalt therapy will reveal how far that is a myth for anyone, how much our choices may be constrained in ways that are outside awareness. And as awareness grows, the gestalt belief is that all we choose to do becomes more rewarding to the doer and to whom and what forms her context.

One of Perls' important new ideas about human nature was his insistence that our behaviour comes from needs, rather than instincts or drives. These needs are activated by emotion, which in its root meaning means no more than mover, that which moves. Like Abraham Maslow, he saw these needs emerging in a hierarchy, the most urgent first. An extreme example might be of a deer stopping grazing and fleeing a lion; then at a certain moment it has to stop to recover breath, even though the lion is near. The need to breathe comes at the top of the hierarchy. So, from the beginning of life, the whole organism of the person in her environment is seen in gestalt to be in a ceaseless and productive process of identifying needs, bringing them to awareness where necessary, and so allowing them to be fulfilled.

Field theory

By 1947 Perls had written his first book (1969[1947]) on his new understandings. He struggled to find a name for this therapy, and for a time called it concentration therapy. This referred to the method, which was to concentrate on the present. With his wife Laura, he finally chose the title gestalt. This German word, not obvious in pronunciation to English speakers, means, roughly, pattern, or organisation, or pattern-forming. It is an oblique reference to the field theory put forward by Kurt Lewin. Lewin was a social psychologist with high awareness of how human behaviour is a function of the field, of the person and her context. In his own exact but wordy description: 'a field is defined as the totality of coexisting facts which are conceived of as mutually interdependent' (1951: 240). He also warned: 'It is particularly necessary that one who proposes to study whole-phenomena should guard against the tendency to make wholes as all-embrasive as possible' (Ellis 1938: 289). The way this 'totality of coexisting facts' form a pattern or gestalt, a fleeting organised whole in anyone's mind, seemed always to reveal a foreground need against the background that had created it. Field theory thus became one of the major shapers of this new theory.

Similar ideas came from gestalt psychology, which struck Perls as a true description of perception. This was a German nineteenth-century movement. Max Wertheimer was among the first to suggest that we perceive in what could be called meaningful wholes (Ellis 1938: 2). According to our need at the time, we organise a selection of data into a dynamic pattern or gestalt. So, a gestalt is a whole that is greater than the sum of its parts.

This is perhaps easier to follow in examples than just as an idea. Think of the score of a piece of music. It is not difficult to count how many quavers, minims and so on, and achieve the sum of the parts that make up, say, a movement of a symphony. But it is the organisation of those notes, their sequence and pattern, that becomes the symphony itself. The whole is greater than the sum of its parts. A symphony is the outcome of not only a talent but a need in the composer to produce a statement that to many people will be very beautiful, or in some special way significant. The whole is an integration of the parts that make it up, rather than a mere collection of them. A nineteenth-century banker, Charles Ephrussi, described a work of art as 'a luminous unity whose separate elements melt together into an indivisible whole' (De Waal 2010: 78). That was his inspiring perception. In a sense, every gestalt is an ephemeral work of art formed by whoever perceives it. It too can be a luminous entity, whose separate elements have melted together into an indivisible whole. Yet this whole is not static.

Embedded here are more inferences we can make about human nature. One is about pleasure in the aesthetic or what some people term the spiritual. This is something that defies much academic measuring but is emotionally real. There seems to be some locus of recognition in most of us, of what we variously perceive as a fine person or building or sunset or picture or piece of behaviour. But we do not all appreciate everything the same way at all. What is more, we have our own sense of when any work of art is complete. If the musicians suddenly stop playing before the last bar of our symphony, the discomfort in the audience will be great. There is a **tendency to completion** in our minds. We need to make something of it, in the common phrase, in this instance meaning to give a complete shape to whatever we are perceiving. Ovsianka (1928(2): 302–89) described this human tendency both to complete actions and percepts, as well to return to the unfinished. From the uncrossed 't' in a piece of writing, to the never yet delivered message of farewell or love, the unfinished seems to nag or produce unease until it is dealt with.

An easy illustration of this is when I feel hungry. I may be called to the phone, have to catch the post, or for a thousand reasons need to postpone eating. But that need will come back in lively fashion for most of us, until satisfied, when the whole subject of food loses vibrancy. Done and dusted. For the time it has gone.

Where and when I feel hungry is highly significant. In a city street, I can play with the idea of a cafe or sandwich shop or grocery as a way of dealing with my need. How much I want to spend is also part of the gestalt, and how long I have free, and much besides. In other words, I deal with my need for food according to outer realities as well as inner ones, such as a loathing of white bread, or a special wish for cheese at that moment. My need is shaped by the environment. It cannot be separated from the environment, just as I cannot be separated from the environment. So, as already stated, the gestalt view of human nature is of its indivisibility from whatever surrounds us. And we are group animals, so we are always, in our minds if not physically, in relation to people. It is said that all action is reaction. As gestalt therapy has developed, more and more attention has been given to how what happens between people is generally a co-creation, modified by both or all.

In some psychodynamic training, the conductor of a small group will comment on whatever happens as coming from 'part of the group'. It can be difficult for some members ever to acknowledge that what they do is a function of the field represented by that group. In an individualistic society, the myth is of separateness. That is a small illustration of the gestalt understanding, shared with Freudian thinkers, that the group may be acting through us as much as we are acting upon the group.

In much of what is called Western society, the idea of individuality is prized. So a notion of being dependent on, entwined, or embedded in anything may be inimical. Over recent years the indivisibility of people and their environment has been hotly disputed. Are we causing or accelerating global warming? Would it happen anyway? Whatever the answer, the consequence is the same. There is no way that we can forever rise above climate change and the natural disasters and food shortages that follow. If the planet goes, we go.

Choice

In gestalt, the therapist seeks to raise her awareness and enable the client to raise his, in the expectation that the client will then have a larger repertoire of responses available to him. In other words, he will have more choice. Fields of data in his mind will enlarge or alter, and will form new gestalts, new patterns. All this is a function of now, of the present. This optimistic therapy emphasises making choices that are energising and life-enhancing. One theoretical background to this is in existentialism, which is a strong influence in gestalt therapy theory. As far back as 1843 Kierkegaard, often called the father of existentialism, put forward the idea, still insisted on in gestalt therapy, of each person being responsible for his or her own actions. About eighty years later Martin Buber (1970 [1922]) added to this idea his insistence that the fundamental fact of human nature is relationship, experienced in **the between** of I and Thou.

Now, the present, is when contact happens. This belief is likewise intrinsic to this therapy. How data emerge into awareness, which is always the present, is for the gestalt therapist an indication of how to meet and work with the client. Merleau-Ponty enriched the philosophy with the depth of his thinking about phenomenology, while Husserl and Sartre are other existentialists of the first part of the twentieth century who recognised that we are all born into constraint, into places, times and histories which limit us. But alongside these constraints, we largely make our lives ourselves, by our choices. Every choice tends either towards stagnation and curtailment, or to what we are talking about here, excitement and growth.

John came to therapy complaining of the unbearable selfishness of his wife. They were short of money and she was refusing to return to work after having their first child. Over many sessions he came to see that much of his anger was to do with how he had been a latch-key child, and felt huge jealousy of his baby who, in his words, would have a cushy time of it. Accepting this hitherto unacceptable and unacknowledged feeling in himself was enough to let him change to a different perception. His feelings changed, his behaviour changed, and he became supportive of his wife and loving of his child.

A major choice John had made was to admit something uncomfortable, rather than hold the cause of his bad feelings out of awareness. The spontaneous change that followed gave him a whole range of freer and more creative choices than those he had given himself while he was feeling punitive. The nature of this change he experienced is described at greater length in the chapter on theory. The point here is the expansion of choice following on his own changed perception, and not because it was guided by anyone else's sense of what he should feel or do.

Wholehearted action is understood in gestalt, as by many observant people, to come from a sound choice made by the enacter. At a perhaps regrettable level, we see how much advertising is designed not just to tell the worth of a product, but to persuade the buyer to want it, as the kind of life-enhancement that all choices at best are. The buyer's belief is sought. This belief, perhaps better described as a sense of rightness for oneself, is what John came to in the vignette here.

Most of our understandings of human nature are based on observation and our personal experience, and are therefore still assumptions that may be upheld or disproved, perhaps, as neuroscience advances. So it has to be an assumption in gestalt that humans are as profoundly social as this therapy believes. The powerful assumption here is that where people make choices which greatly enlarge awareness, those choices will be social. This means that individualistic gratification at the expense of others is a distortion, in some ways doing as much harm to the doer as to the done-to. This statement is more explicit than in many existentialist writings. Noticing your own responses as you read it may tell you a good deal.

You may by now begin to see gestalt as optimistic, with a belief in a tendency to health, order and social survival, if people respond to their own central awareness rather than just to the rules of society. It defines psychological health in terms of fluent gestalt formation, the uninterrupted registering and dealing appropriately with new experience. I hope that these ideas, including the notion of constant change and dynamism, will be new enough to many readers to warrant this introductory chapter.

Developmental theory and gestalt

People develop. Earlier in this chapter I spoke of some of the dramatic changes we go through in the womb. Infancy is still a period of very rapid growth and learning, about which there have been theories no doubt since Neanderthal times. In the nineteenth century, the slogan 'Spare the rod and spoil the child' was an excuse for the punitive, and a troublesome imperative to the tender-hearted parent. If children were born bad, then goodness was to be trained, beaten, into them. In the early twentieth century the Truby King system of infant rearing required rigid time boundaries. Baby was to be fed every four hours, and left to roar between whiles if she so wished. Later that century demand feeding became the fashion, with bottle or breast proffered whenever the infant grew restless. In other words, the mother was not to have any demands of her own. Very contrary pictures of what babies, what people, are like, are evident in such different regimes. The first suggests that discipline is to be taught rigidly, from without. The second suggests that the baby knows what she wants, and must be respected in that, without regard to any other needs in the people round her.

Perls, Hefferline and Goodman (1951 [hereafter PHG]) made clear in this early book about gestalt therapy that, in their view, the needs of any one person are never separable from the whole context of where, when and with whom in the world they occur. The phrase co-creation has been coined since their time, and is used to describe the negotiation that is implicit in a great deal of human interaction. They saw us primarily as social animals. To them this meant, as already stated in this chapter, that where there is sufficient awareness, everything we do will be socially acceptable. This is different from saying we ought to or should behave in particular ways.

In gestalt, true selfishness is in the gratification of one without deprivation of another. A true yet difficult example of this truth is of a nun I met who was sent to work in a Brazilian slum and could not bear to eat enough herself while she saw people who were not only hungry but sick. She was sent home for failing to understand that she would be of no use as a nurse if she was starving and ill herself. This illustration is rather of how deprivation of one will not in this case make for gratification of the many. One person might have eaten better on her food. The whole group needed her medical skills more than her individual sacrifice of her health and strength.

Later theorists have refined and expanded the idea of our being social animals from the beginning of life. Psychologists had once supposed that young babies had very low awareness of other people, or rather, of whether anything was outside or inside them.

Daniel Stern (1985) was a specially gifted experimenter with infants and their carers, who deduced that recognition and learning from the other begin as we are born, and before. The early gestalt therapy theorists also assumed that infants learn relationally, in contact with the other, who is more often than not the mother in many early interactions. Perls was fascinated with the stages of nourishment in early months and years, and suggested that what is learned by each of us in these stages can influence how we take in learning for the rest of our lives.

Some people, for example, tend to wait, to be dependent, doing more demanding than giving. He saw those as sucklings, who for whatever reason have not finished with that stage of life, but go on seeking symbolically to re-create it. Then there are the unwilling feeders, holding unfamiliar experience at bay and living in a less nourished way as a result. Then there are the counter-dependent, that he characterised by the hanging-on bite, that hurts the other and does not free the biter to wider experience. Weaning he saw as moving into a more proactive way of life, symbolically leading to the capacity to get out there, to choose, seek, be curious and to discriminate more and more, before assimilating experience.

All this adds up to a recognition of development, and a suggestion that it is useful for therapists to have stages of early life in mind when talking to adult clients. Two major theorists on human development have influenced later gestalt, and are very often incorporated into training. They are Daniel Stern, already mentioned, and John Bowlby. Their theories and their contribution to this one are explained more in Chapter Six.

Competition

The theories of Stern and Bowlby stress the co-operation that is an important part of the development of human nature. Competition is very evidently also part of how we are. In some modern educational systems it has been seen as bad for all those who do not win. And the designated losers would probably agree.

Perls saw competition as at best an evolutionary force, a striving to do as well or better than has been done yet. After the 4-minute mile or the record marathon, the endeavour seems to be to beat the time, rather than beat the person who achieved the first record. In this sense, researchers are in constant competition with bacteria and viruses, racing to find ways to combat the constant modifications of these minute creatures. In Perls' view, competition only goes wrong when it is what he called neurotic. By this he meant when it is about doing down another person, rather than emulating and improving knowledge or a skill.

Anger

The early writers saw this feature of human nature to have two major forms that they called red or white. In red anger, the frustration is about loss of closeness, and the whole underlying urge is to clear the way to re-establishing good contact. In white anger, the frustration has rigidified into a wish to annihilate who or whatever is the frustrater.

Because anger is so often unacceptable, it can be the work of a therapist to raise awareness of it in a client. At one time there was a stereotype of gestalt therapy as an anger-inciting, cushion-beating cathartic process. The reality is that anger is very often associated with impotence, with a perceived lack of power to do or have what is wished. The gestalt belief is in the wisdom of the organism. If I let myself be aware of what I need or want, and find how to achieve it, then anger becomes an irrelevant emotion. Catharsis, the sudden release of pent-up and often unacknowledged feelings of many kinds, can be a strong and important event in anyone's life. It may happen in gestalt therapy, but insight may make it unnecessary.

Aggression

This word commonly lives as a neighbour of the word anger. But in its derivation it means no more than outwardly-directed activity. It is in this latter sense that Perls used it in the title of his first book. Part of his thesis was that enacting rather than brooding or retroflecting, taking action rather than complaining and doing nothing, would lead to a somewhat saner world. He alleged that awareness and loss of fear make for straightforward communication between people.

What we call civilised society often involves white lies, suppression of honest responses if they are negative, and so to a build-up of tiny frustrations that ultimately find outlets in such dramatic ways as torture, murder, or war. 'Finally there has to be a political solution,' the politicians regularly and self-righteously proclaim, after doing their best to annihilate some power they see as threatening. By this they mean that people will have to sit down and talk, to come away from white anger and to make as good an accommodation as the context will allow. People will need to be in contact.

So we are at full circle of thinking about gestalt theory and human nature. Awareness and contact are at the heart of our needs, unless we feel our lives are threatened. In the next chapter we look more closely at the theory that has evolved in gestalt from these recognitions of human nature.

Summary

In a last analysis, there may not be too many conclusions to come to about human nature. So the good ideas of one school of thought are likely to chime with those of another. Perls himself, talking about the different schools of psychotherapy, said, 'All are right, but some are right-eous.' And it does seem difficult for many of us not to make possessions of ideas, claiming that they belong to this or that first publicist of them.

Experiment

With a colleague or by yourself if need be, take a few minutes to recall some of the most surprising bits of theory about human nature that you have ever been told. Then say what your own belief is in that area.

TWO

Theory of Gestalt Counselling

The theory itself is grounded in experience and observation; it has grown and changed with years of practice and application, and it is still growing. (Perls 1978: xiii)

Gestalt theory ... demands that we stay close to the facts and repudiate descriptions leading to artificialities. (Kohler in Ellis 1938: 57)

The counsellor's task

My job as a gestalt counsellor is to raise awareness. As we sit together, my awareness of the client and his difficulties will grow by the minute, and my task will be to notice and respond to how he changes his awareness. [In this book I shall, for convenience, usually refer to counsellors as feminine gender, and clients as masculine.]

I am not there to persuade the client to cheer up or buck up or change his general behaviour in any way. It may well be that if he comes to notice and accept, from moment to moment, more of the reality of how he creates his present perceptions, that in itself will enable him to change. It seems upside down to say that accepting what is now is a key to being different. Maybe that is why this idea, central in gestalt, is called the **paradoxical theory of change** (Beisser 1970). Awareness is concerned with the whole of the client, and the whole of the scene in which he is, at this moment and in his life.

So, gestalt is **holistic**. A co-founder of the Paris School of Gestalt uses a pentagram to represent this holism, the points of the star representing heart, head, body, society and world (Ginger 2003: 23).

A young woman came to see me some years ago, saying she was very stressed. She was pale and seemed under-nourished, and fidgeted with her hands a good deal. She spoke in a thin, tight voice, saying she wanted to relax. I said I kept noticing how she seemed to be wringing the fingers of one hand with the other. She pursed her lips and said she wanted some relaxation exercises. They had never worked before but she hoped I could make them work, though she doubted it. I reported to her, smiling, that I was momentarily scared when she flushed and pursed her lips. 'I didn't,' she said quickly, than after a pause, 'Did I? And I scared you?' As she took in this tiny exchange, her shoulders dropped, and her voice softened. She had let herself admit how she could be with other people, and she spontaneously changed. Beisser's theory had been demonstrated.

Here and now

Staying with what is present is a major part of gestalt theory and practice. Fritz Perls, the founder, sometimes said **the therapist's task is to frustrate every effort the client makes to escape the present**. So we need to be clear about what he meant by the present, the now. It could be argued that the room where you are sitting is much of your present at the moment. Or perhaps the words you are reading have tuned out for the moment the place where you are. Or, if you have been told to read this before a class, and if you are going to a party tonight, images of friends, clothes, dances, will keep surging into awareness, as you perhaps tell yourself to buy a bottle, iron some garment, and take a CD with you.

This imagined party is in the future. Yet needs and imaginings to do with it may make up recurrent moments of your now, if you are excited about the coming event, or, more probably, about the people you will see there. In gestalt theory, then, whatever is occupying your awareness is, for you, the present.

Defining now

We all use this word with wide meanings. 'Do it now!' really means do it as soon as possible, as now has slipped away with the utterance. Then there is a general now, akin to nowadays, the general present, as in saying that many people now carry mobiles. In gestalt, now is more highly focused. Martin Buber spoke of the narrow ridge, forever changing or flowing between past and future. In that sense now is always ungraspable.

Daniel Stern is a writer who is trained in psychiatry rather than gestalt, but whose brilliant contributions to research and theory have influenced our recent understandings. He suggests that what we all do all the time is shape our time into bites of a few seconds, each being a complete little now or gestalt in itself. He thinks that these moments typically last between four and ten seconds (Stern 2004: 55). He calls them lived stories, emotional unfoldings that can be likened to musical phrases. He echoes this therapy in his insistence that paying attention to these nows is immensely important. Catching now is harder than catching butterflies, and as destructive. So it is perhaps enough just to notice how ephemeral it is.

Gestalt formation

Only connect. Relatedness is all. Perhaps the most important relatedness in life generally, and in therapy, is that between people. In gestalt theory that place or moment of meeting is called the **contact-boundary**. It is an abstract way of describing how we meet and react to each other. At every level we are made of each other. Before moving on to that central area of gestalt theory, I want to talk of how whatever we perceive is in a **field** or **context**, a **background** to the **foreground** that is in awareness. These words are in bold, to show their importance in gestalt theory.

Kurt Lewin was a psychologist who invented field theory, the idea, perhaps obvious to you, or perhaps even unwelcome, that we cannot be separated from our context (Lewin 1951). Perls often used the rather cumbersome word **organism** to mean a person. He, like Lewin, insisted that **organism and environment are indivisible** (PHG 1951). Environment in this sense means whatever the organism or person is dealing with at the time. So the environment is often another person or group, as well as a ham sandwich or a flood. In this way, gestalt counselling has always been concerned with relatedness and with systems.

The method is often concerned with shedding light on the background, the context which the client, more aware of the foreground, may be ignoring. Let us take a concrete route to explaining this. One person may hold a very different context or background for the same foreground. A yachtsman looking at the sea is probably as aware of the wind as of the water. His pressing need is for control of his boat, and that need organises his field of perception. A small child on holiday sees the biggest paddling pool ever, and races to reach it. Her need is for the grand work of early childhood, sensual experience, activity, discovery. Her big sister is watching the promenade, and waiting for young men to appear and admire her bikini and the glorious tan she has just rubbed into her skin. Each of these three makes of the seaside what his or her needs decide. In gestalt jargon, each configures the field with a different foreground. They make quite different patterns or organisations of the same data.

Going back to our student party-goer, we could say that she has not managed to organise her day so that she can relax into it. The reading has been imposed on her, and the shops are going to shut, and she seems not to be sure that she will remember the CD. In other words, several needs are jostling for attention inside her, and she is not dealing with any of them in a way that leaves them done and dusted. You have possibly already solved her difficulties in your own mind, perhaps by putting the CD in her coat pocket, buying the bottle now, doing the ironing and then finishing one chapter of reading. In terms of theory, you have imagined completing several gestalts. You have tracked a path from stimulus or arousal, through excitation, imagining solutions, or what to do, then doing it and feeling a little glow of achievement or relief. Somewhere in that is food for learning, for taking on board what to do better next time. You are at rest again, ready for the next gestalt to form.

The cycle of experience

In an early work, *Ego, Hunger and Aggression*, Perls described this process of gestalt formation. He said that first a disturbing factor interrupts the state of rest (Perls 1969[1947]: 43). It can be from within, like the student's worries about the party, or from outside, like the sea entering the consciousness of the people we just talked of. Joseph Zinker (1978) elaborated this description into what he called the cycle of experience. In his version, the disturbing factor is inevitably a sensory stimulus; it is something felt or heard or seen or tasted or smelt. It, or rather the person experiencing it, becomes emotionally charged. Then the whole organism, not necessarily the brain, decides what to do about it, and the body does it. The sense of finishing comes next, and learning, even at the simple level of whether that was a course of action worth repeating or never to touch with a barge pole again. Once more the organism is at rest, if the cycle has happened without interruption.

The cycle of experience is a model of a dynamic event and, like all models, it is necessarily false, as it is not the real thing. Later writers have modified the model. Neuroscience supports the idea that something like these cycles happens constantly, outside awareness as well as inside it. And as neuroscience develops, we shall undoubtedly find a more exact model of gestalt formation and enactment.

The unfinished gestalt

If I do not find a way to deal with my need satisfactorily, the gestalt cycle does not go through smoothly and disappear without a squeak. It looks as if the unfulfilled need instead tries another way of pushing for attention. Perls once proclaimed that we all re-enact our major conflicts every thirty seconds. He was encouraging therapists to notice all the details of a client's behaviour, be it hesitation, mumbling or any of a hundred other voice variations. Gestures and little sequences of actions are just as likely to be a person's habitual way of letting some steam out of a need which is pressing. It may be one he does not want or perhaps dare to fulfil openly, or it may be implicit, so disturbing that it has been excluded from awareness.

Existential phenomenology

A major curse of counselling and psychotherapy is long words. Unfortunately some big brutes enter here. Van Dusen (Pursglove 1968: 29–41) was early on the scene in describing Gestalt therapy as, at its simplest, *dasein*, or being-here analysis. So far so good. The longer words around this are commonly used, so I present them, with apologies. They are existential-phenomenology. The roots of both halves of this portmanteau word are interesting, and complicated. In our context, it is enough to note that existentialism, a philosophy that calls Kirkegaard its father, is interpreted in many ways. In gestalt, it is to do with the emphasis on present experience, and on individual responsibility for the choices that make a rich or a more impoverished life (van Deurzen 2010).

Phenomenology is similarly a word that is perhaps two inches wide, but a mile deep. It is to do with reaching the essence, the truth, via subjective experience. In gestalt it describes exploring the nature of experience itself. The phenomenology of Merleau-Ponty (1962), which holds that consciousness is intersubjective, describes this in detail. It is such an important part of gestalt practice that the whole of the next chapter of this book is devoted to it.

The self

The word self is used often in gestalt theory. This small syllable stands for very different meanings for different schools of philosophy and psychology. Self is partly seen as a sense of self, derived from the system of contacts at any time. In the central 1951 text, the writers talk of the **self as image**, and the **self as function**. Self as an image is in some ways a myth, a concept of being Me, who could never do some bad act or other, or who is fascinatingly subject to allergies, or who in a myriad ways has made an **enduring self-description**, which may or may not have much to do with anyone else's experience.

Self as function means such involvement in the present, in the scene one is in, in the truth of one's own responses, that what you or I are doing is so intense that there is at any moment in some way less sense of self than of **engagement in what is happening**. This idea, now being adopted by many schools of counselling and other thinkers, is expanded in the next section.

Contact

According to gestalt theory, if we all surged along completing these so-called cycles of experience as the stimuli occurred, humans would be a good deal more fulfilled than they often are now. We would be making **full contact**. This means achieving a very strong sense of what or whom engages us at that moment, so that we respond in a way that is right for us. Perls first called his new therapy concentration therapy, as a way of describing the full presence in the moment that he believed to be true psychological health. He believed in an ability within each of us to recognise and act on what in Buddhist thought is called 'right action'.

The poet Shelley said that in the moment of inspiration, the mind is a fading coal. Rather in the same way, Perls suggested that in such a moment of what he called **full contact**, the self is a fading coal. For that second or two, I am the action, the meeting, the discovery. The title of his major work has the strap line, 'Excitement and Growth in the Human Personality'. He saw full contact as the means to that growth and excitement.

In everyday language, which existed long before psychology was made into a formal study, we speak of being taken out of ourselves when fully engaged in what we are doing. This is a central mystery of being. We are most ourselves, very often, when self-forgetful, whether absorbed in a puzzle, or another person, a sunset, or a house on fire.

Part of the delight of much sport is the high concentration needed, so that speed and accuracy of response are for moments the whole of life. Total involvement, or full contact, seems to be something we seek. With people, there can be instants of meeting that seem like a momentary fusion of love or understanding or synchronicity of thought. Martin Buber described these rare moments of being truly person to person as **I–Thou**. More recently, Daniel Stern has written of the intense responsiveness that we all have to each other. There is more about this intersubjective awareness in the chapter on dialogue.

Perls said of true meeting between people, 'contact involves what the other actually is, not what one construes him to be' (1978: 56). So the experience of full contact is self-as-function, as I described it in the last section.

Here I want to show how what we call contact, the here and now meeting experience, is a remarkably important part of life, and of counselling. It is how I live. If I half-look at, half-grasp what is there, I miss the full impact of the experience, as a Christmas visit I once witnessed made clear.

Uncle Ted, visiting his sister's family, was asked to tell the children about his adventures in Africa. He demurred, then began to give a dry account of a political uprising. He looked into the middle distance, and twice stopped until an older child urged him on. The bored younger ones began to nudge each other, and then wrestle. Uncle glanced at them impatiently and asked to be reminded where he was in the story. The scene ended when the younger children knocked over the fire irons and one began to scream, Ted's sister arrived and, you may be sure, a more dramatic scene soon began.

If we look just at Uncle Ted, it seems that he did not really want to tell the story, or more likely, he did not want to tell a children's story, so he did not. He did not make full contact with his own response when the father suggested the story, or he would have said no. So he chose to go along, to be **confluent** with the suggestion, rather perhaps than be seen as rude. Then he did not stay in contact with either the children or with what he was saying, as they were well aware. The younger ones soon found a more riveting instant contact in nudging and pulling each other about.

This is a very slight example of someone being out of contact with his own responses, so he makes a half-hearted job of something, and satisfaction is hard to find anywhere in the scene. Very simply, we all need to be in touch enough to say yes or say no to what we want or are asked to do. We need to be in touch with our own central unconflicted response. Since we are indivisible from our surroundings, these will strongly influence what we choose to do. What happened here seems to be over-influenced by the surroundings of the visit, and under-influenced by the needs of Uncle Ted.

Many people who come to counselling have shut off this precious self-reference, probably for excellent reasons, in their early life. Gestalt counselling will partly be concerned with letting them make contact with *how* they do this shutting off. Uncle Ted conveniently illustrates some of these operations.

Awareness

It looks as if he managed not to register awarely that the children were making a noise. But something got through, enough to make him lose the thread of the story. He, like all of us, could tune out a sensory impact.

That cut-off is at the gateway to the person, where the senses register. In healthy gestalt formation, a quickening happens after the sensory impact, an excitement that probably registers in awareness as feeling. Uncle Ted's story was devoid of feeling, and that probably led to the children's rejection of it.

Another thing that happens when things are going well is that the person hits on a satisfying way of meeting his own needs and the needs and potentiality of the environment. This may seem subtle, but most of us do it wonderfully, all day long, with occasional disastrous lapses. If I am hungry in a town, I may well decide to go into a cafe or buy a bun. If I am hungry in a jungle, it will do me little good to wonder whether Starbucks or Pret is my choice of the day.

Now it looks as if Uncle Ted was not in touch with what he wanted. Or perhaps he was, and that was what kept getting in the way of his story and making him stop. But in either case, telling that story to that audience was a poor solution, as it satisfied nobody. With awareness, he might have changed his decision, or changed his story to suit children. A good second best to an unsuccessful action is to see that it does not work, and start again. Once again, Uncle Ted was out of touch, and ploughed forward until the clanging fire-irons testified to an honest response from the young.

Contact involves being in touch with your needs, in the field of who you are and where you are. It means making a **creative adjustment** between the needs in you and the circumstances around you. We do not know, but can guess at a possible creative adjustment for Uncle Ted. Rather than give in to the demand for a story, and in that way try to please only what was outside himself, he might have done his card tricks, thus entertaining the children and himself.

After contact there is a relaxing, a finishing, and with luck a learning of whether what you said or did could be improved on, repeated, or never touched again with a barge-pole. This learning from experience has the potential to begin change from one minute episode, to within a lifetime, over millennia, indeed aeons, as history and pre-history show. It is a process which has, as just one example, brought about the interactive miracle of human speech. It is a personal and a social learning, as it is pretty little use if there is only one of you.

Autonomy and response-ability

While thinking about the interactive and intersubjective nature of most human activity, a word on Perls' concept of autonomy is needed. Laura and Fritz Perls stressed self-reliance, autonomy, as highly desirable. They had lived through the Nazi regime, and must have been acutely aware of the danger of confluent following, of introjecting the racist messages that came from that. They wanted the locus of authority to be inside individuals. Paul Goodman is widely seen as the writer of Perls' ideas in the major work of 1951. He was a proponent of anarchic thinking, who had considerable influence on the libertarian, flower-power movement of the seventies (Goodman 1960, Stoehr 1994). Indivisible as we all are from our political and social context, it is not surprising that they stressed autonomy to such a degree that, in Perls' case at least, it sounded at times as if he advocated a complete disregard for the field, the background, the rest of the world. Their equal stress on field theory, contact and awareness runs counter to this reading. Nevertheless, modern gestalt thinking shows much more excitement about intersubjectivity, with its emphasis on co-creation, than did the founders.

Both concepts are important. In an individualistic society the stress on intersubjectivity is needed. In regimes that oppress free thinking – and the world abounds in them – autonomy deserves every encouragement.

An important part of this idea of autonomy is that everyone is responsible for his or her actions. The underlying assumption in gestalt counselling is that the more anyone is aware, the more responsible or response-able she becomes. Response-able is a useful re-writing of an old word. It says that the more I really notice, the less experience I tune out, the larger the repertoire of responses I have.

Theory of change

Near the beginning of this chapter I spoke of the paradoxical theory of change, which states that change will come about when what is now is fully accepted. Barry Stevens wrote a book called *Don't Push the River* (2005), which is another way of expressing the same idea. Carl Rogers' person-centred therapy has the same idea implicit in it.

The impasse

This acceptance of what is may not be easy. If I have built the story of my life round my father's sudden death when I was nineteen, and believed that that explained my stormy marriage and abandonment of a child, it is likely to be horribly expensive to my image of myself, or in other words, shaming, to let myself see, perhaps, that I was an angry rebel from long before that, and had other large family conflicts.

This vignette is a disguised memory of a young client we can call Sue, whose progress in therapy clearly showed some of Perls' theory of the potential stages of the change process. She first told her story fluently and even defiantly. When I did not challenge it, she suggested that I was not a very good therapist. Thinking back over a career, and remembering the many misunderstandings and other mistakes I have made, I could agree with her here too. By the next session she was angry with her ex-husband. I let myself comment that she was talking much more about other people than about herself, and that none of them seemed acceptable. After more sessions she faced an empty chair in which she imagined her husband, and railed at him forcefully. Invited to change places and speak from his point of view, she froze, seeming to lose herself. I said it looked as if she was really stopping herself. She burst into sobs, and gradually admitted the painful insights she was having, and the huge emotional reversal she was experiencing when she let into her mind the idea of what someone else might be experiencing.

The moment she lost herself, froze, or as she said later, felt as if she was in a black void, she was in what Perls called the **impasse**. He recognised it as a sign of imminent change, where other therapists might just have been worried that the client was upset, and steered her back from the brink of discovery. Perls saw the impasse as connected to the fertile void, the still place where prejudice has not intruded, and new or yet unadmitted perceptions can suddenly blossom.

Because the paradoxical theory of change is much talked of in gestalt, others may be overlooked. For example, Aristotle said that the earliest form of learning is **imitation**. In therapy that is going to happen, often under the more respectable label of modelling. The counsellor will focus awareness on if and how she is imitated, and comment. Another path to change that is intrinsic to gestalt is through **experiment**. Experiment and dialogue are two major methods in gestalt therapy, and they will both have chapters of their own in this book. Here it is enough to say that many experiments bring about change. Experiments serve different purposes, among them, giving an opportunity for the client to invent a new way of dealing with the world, to imagine and enact a new creative adjustment.

Polarities

A phenomenon appreciated in gestalt for its therapeutic relevance is polarity, our tendency to fragment or split rather than achieve a unified perception. 'On the one hand or on the other', 'My heart says this and my head says that'. The dilemmas in these common expressions speak of incomplete gestalt formation, of discomfort and unfulfilment. Ought and want are often the two sides of such a conflict. Perls called them top dog and under dog. Top dog is sometimes morality, conscience, correctness, super-ego. Under dog is nearer id, the apparently more selfish gratification. He suggested that the under dog generally wins, in the sense of frustrating the top dog. The chapter on experiment has much to say about polarities.

The muddle about who is who

Every therapy has its way of describing the ways people frustrate themselves, and often other people too. As I describe these gestalt concepts of what others would call defence or resistance, you may see why I chose this heading. On the face of it I, and perhaps you, feel pretty clear about the fact that I am I and you are you. At first it is often easier to spot other people doing what in gestalt theory are called **introjecting** or **projecting** or **retroflecting**. Let's look at these ideas in turn. In our theory they are more often nowadays seen first as styles of behaving, rather than pathologised and labelled as unhealthy. The early gestaltists saw them more as what they called interruptions to contact.

Introjection and developmental theory

Introjection means swallowing whole, taking in without criticism or examination. Perls' theory of the aetiology, the origin, of most problematic ways of being is to do with eating, as I described in Chapter 1. Freud linked neurosis to sexuality, particularly as it forms in infancy. Perls argued that eating is a yet more fundamental human need and activity than sex. He traced our beginning from the time we were all sucklings, only taking in milk, and at that stage needing to be introjectors, needing to swallow whole. This sort of introjection is vital to life. The occasional troubled baby who does not want to suck is at risk of dying.

Most of us move from uncritical taking in milk, to starting solid food, getting teeth, and beginning to discriminate about what to eat and how to eat it, as most parents are painfully aware as the spoonsful of spinach hit their shirts. The baby is learning a new survival skill, of being able to distinguish good food from what is unfamiliar or may be harmful. Very often, what is unfamiliar is at first rejected. At best, the great variety of food that suits us omnivorous humans comes to be accepted, chewed thoroughly, with the pips and fish-bones and gristle removed, then swallowed and assimilated. This is what Perls saw as the healthy way of not only eating but taking in experience generally throughout life.

Most of us turn out to hold on to some habit of introjecting. Perhaps out of awareness, most of us seem to know this and act on it. Just look at people meeting a baby or toddler. They are very likely assuring the baby that he is beautiful, bright, lovely, clever, or a host of other most complimentary adjectives. It is as if the speaker wants the baby to introject these enhancing ideas, and the baby usually joins in, smiling and wriggling at the compliments.

But not only happy ideas are offered to most of us about who we are or how we should behave. At school I had to learn and frequently repeat the phrase, 'Forgive others often, myself never.' It took me a long time to decide not to keep myself in a class apart from the rest of the world, as the only unforgivable person.

Many people introject far harsher rules, suggestions and ideas. In terms of gestalt theory, they are stuck at the suckling stage of development. They have not evolved into biting off, chewing over and generally discriminating what they will accept and what they will reject from the messages given to them.

A young man came to me for therapy, complaining of being very, indeed embarrassingly, clumsy. Soon he reported that his father had always told him he was a complete fool, and he knew he was. As he said this, he managed to knock over a small table beside his chair. 'You see?'

he said. I thanked him for showing me his symptom so clearly. He stopped blushing and began to laugh. I grinned. We both seemed to have seen the Chaplinesque possibilities of our meeting. Perhaps he would break the chair next, or swing on the light and tear it out of the ceiling. As our meetings progressed, the young man came to understand how he had swallowed whole the message that he was a fool. And he decided that what showed as clumsiness was both obedience to his father's judgement and punishment of that same person for being so destructive. He could imagine the table or other dropped or kicked objects as that very father, or at least the side of the father that could be so harsh.

In theory terms, he undid or reversed the retroflection, by seeing that he was getting back at the father as the father had got at him. And he understood that all this was to do with what you could call the historic father, the young father with money worries and an ill wife and a frightening boss, someone quite unlike the quiet widower he had become in later age. The young man began to notice how he tensed his whole body and seemed almost to will himself to drop cups or step backwards onto dogs. As he let in this awareness, he gradually changed, until he reported that he had carried a tray of drinks successfully, without even worrying that he would do otherwise.

Confluence is a state described in gestalt theory. In Latin it means flowing together. It is part of retroflection, as we have just seen. And it is frequent in everyday life. Sometimes it is gratifying, if it leads to a simultaneous response. But I sometimes find myself agreeing with the last speaker, without forming a view of my own, or obeying some gesture of command from someone, against my better judgement. As a therapist you need to be on the alert for what may seem like co-operation from someone, but turns out to be blind acceptance. Assimilation is the word meaning proper chewing and digesting. Unless a client has assimilated the therapist's responses, the therapist might as well save her breath to cool her porridge.

Transference and projection

Projection is doing what a cinema projector does: send an image from itself so that it is noticed in a different place. You probably know people who do this very obviously, like the timid mother who thinks her children are going to be frightened by whatever scares her, or the angry man who thinks everyone is trying to pick a quarrel with him. 'I never shout!' shouts the shouter, 'Tell those people to shut up.'

One Christmas Eve a flood came through the ceiling on to the beds of two small girls. They were left alone in their nightclothes, standing watching the water soak their beds, while their mother ran to the flat above and could be heard hammering on the door. One child rocked and kissed a rag doll, assuring it that everything would be all right and Father Christmas would still come. The other cried silently, stroking her hair forward over her forehead. The owner of the rag doll had projected her urgent need for comfort on to it, and was giving it all the reassurance she surely wanted for herself. And I and everyone I have met do a good deal of projecting, often on to suitable screen people. Projection often involves only seeing what is on the screen, and not realising that it has come from the projector.

In the psychoanalytic school, a major task is to unearth parental transferences, which is the way people project their perceptions of the people significant in their early lives on to current figures, and react accordingly. Perls said you did not need to go to the well when there is a tap in the room. The tap is the present behaviour of the client towards the therapist. The parental transference he saw as having its own importance. And as important in gestalt theory is awakening the client to **how** he repeats the complex process of confluence, introjection, retroflection and projection (Perls 1978: 58).

In modern gestalt practice, the idea of transference has been largely re-admitted. The client's apparent transference on to the therapist, and her counter-transference on to the client, is likely to be looked at both in training and supervision.

Retroflection

The other child in the Christmas Eve flood was doing to herself what she wished that her mother or someone else would do to her. She was stroking and comforting herself, being both the subject and the object of care at the same time. The Latin words in retroflection mean turning back. Most of us do this at times. In this case the retroflection seems useful, as a substitute comfort in a crisis. Perhaps you have seen a child smack himself and say he is bad. This is a sadder retroflection, not of anything he needs done to him but more likely what he thinks a parent wants to do to him.

Retroflection works in two almost opposite ways. The word **proflection** has been added, to help elucidate these different forms of retroflection (Crocker 1981: 13–34). People are also described as retroflecting when they do to themselves what they would like to do to others. Perhaps the boy who smacked himself was of this kind. The clumsy man who had introjected the idea that he was a fool also turned out to be retroflecting his need to punish his father. This need was not even in his awareness, as he blundered and agonised his way through the world, punishing himself instead of another person. Cutting or other self-harm is a retroflection, an action turned back on the doer, rather than being out in the world.

Egotism

Another style or defence that Perls remarked on he called egotism. This is about self-consciousness, in the sense of constantly noticing myself, rather than being totally involved in whatever I am doing. Egotism is about self as image, rather than what I have described as self as function.

The wisdom of the organism

What makes gestalt an optimistic counselling theory is its trust in the wisdom of the organism. This is a belief that as we let ourselves become more aware of our own processes, and the environment, and the web of old habits and fears and introjects Perls called the **maja,** we broaden our range of responses. We become more response-able and responsible, which means more environmentally aware, more creative and more able to grow and develop throughout our lives.

This is the what, some of the theory of gestalt therapy. The rest of this book is about the how.

Experiment

Projection

Sit with someone else and take turns saying what you see as notable parts of their character. After an agreed time, perhaps six or seven minutes, change to seeing what you saw in the other as also a statement about yourself. If you wish, you can make a third phase of this exercise by now telling each other things about yourself that the other did not remark. This may alert you to how strong the element of projection is in our observation of each other.

THREE

Assessment

Phenomenological dialogue, discussed in the next chapter, is the foundation of the gestalt therapy way of making assessments, as well as doing much else. The story the client brings may be foreground for him, and certainly has its own importance. Besides attending to the content of what the client says, the gestalt therapist is alert to what is happening in the behaviour of the client and of herself: in breathing, posture, tension, voice tone, movements, hesitations and the thousand signs we all show each other when we meet, but often disregard as we attend to the content of a story. **Process** is how that story is told.

Sitting behind two women on a bus, I overheard one say somewhat cheerfully, 'Isn't it dreadful? He's going to be off work for weeks, and I'll be the only one in charge. Poor man.' The other lady replied in a subdued, even bored voice, 'Oh, yes, dreadful. Poor man.' She seemed to be responding dutifully to the verbal cues she had been given. I found myself guessing that she was thinking that her friend's manner suggested to her as well as me she might be rather pleased to be the only one in charge. But the second speaker was replying politely to the content of the message, rather than all the other clues in the process, of how that content was delivered.

Gestalt assessment is at best mutual, with both people daring to be more open in their responses to each other than the ladies on the bus. Whether the client seems curious about the therapist already says much about his way of meeting, contacting. A device used by many gestalt therapists is to arrange a first meeting, making it clear that the client will need to go away and reflect on whether to continue working with that therapist, before fixing another appointment. This makes clear that the client is in charge of what happens.

A first task for the therapist is to find how to meet the client, in the sense of tuning in to how he is in the world, rather than making many assumptions. Somebody who finds it difficult to speak may need the meeting to go along very slowly. A hectoring client may need to be met at the same level of energy. The way the client is in the room is of itself full of information for the therapist to read and find a way to respond to. It is a little like a dance in which the therapist does her best to find the right step, rhythm and energy to meet the other. In gestalt language, she is discovering the kind and the depth of contact that will allow the client to begin to feel safe.

To repeat, the therapist sees these early meetings as a chance not just for her to see whether she is ready to work with the client but for the client to find whether he wants to work with her or, indeed, to continue at all. He is a partner in the work. The therapist is not there to prescribe for him but to raise his awareness about his choices, his response-ability.

Working holistically as I have described here, the therapist, as in psychodynamic therapy, does not attempt first to place the client in a diagnostic category. Such categories can be informative, as long as they are not used to reduce the client to a type, rather than respect his uniqueness, his particular way of being agitated or in low spirits or whatever has brought him to the session. An example of a first meeting gives an idea of some of what is needed in beginning an episode of gestalt therapy.

John was referred by his doctor, and arranged this first meeting by phone. In the phone conversation the therapist explained her fee, and said that if John was interested she would like to meet him for one session, after which he could go away and think over whether he wanted to continue, then let her know within a stated time. He agreed, and here he is.

Wilfred Bion said that all therapy starts with two frightened people in a room, and the therapist is aware of her quickened breathing as she introduces herself to this troubled stranger. He is blinking fast, and mumbles his name. She decides to speak first, where with another person she might be moved to wait for the client to begin.

Th.:   As I explained when you rang, this meeting is for us to find out a little about each other, and to see if we are ready to work together.

John: I don't really know what you want me to tell you. I've not had counselling before.

Th.:   I'm remembering some of those television programmes of psychotherapists with X-ray eyes telling patients their pathology and advising eating more bananas or something. [She is aware of wanting to make the conversation more everyday, as she says this]

John: Should I begin with telling you when this all started up?

Th.:   It sounds as if that is what is on your mind. Only I'm feeling nervy. I'm noticing something odd. I'm sitting here worrying about what will make things easier for you, and it sounds as if you are sitting thinking about what I want. [He smiles]

John: We both seem to be thinking of the other person before ourselves. Well my father died when I was eight, and I had two little sisters. And my mother was not a real coper.

Th.:   So that childhood scene sprang into your awareness when I noticed you being so other-centred. I feel a pang to the heart, imagining an eight-year-old ...

John: I thought I was supposed to talk about my childhood.

Th.:   I want to interrupt and explain a bit about how I work. Gestalt, like all therapies, has its own ways, which may seem odd until you have taken them on board. Gestalt is all about awareness, about increasing your awareness, and that is all in the present. So I shall stay as present as I can, and report that, and see if you begin to do the same.

John: [Interrupts] Look, I want to, but I can't stay present like you told me. My problems aren't in this room, they're with my wife.

Th.:   So she is present in your awareness now.

John: So if I think of something, that's present?

Th.:   And so are the sensations and emotions, the memories, the wants, that go with what you think of. Thinking is not all that is going on.

John: Well, as you can imagine, I've had to learn to keep a stiff upper lip. Feelings were not exactly encouraged. So that could be hard. And I'm not quite sure it's worth it. I mean, it keeps everyone happy if I soldier quietly on. [Pause] Is that what you need to know?

Th.:   Thank you for thinking again about what I might need to know.

[There is a long pause]

John: You've hit the nail on the head. I'm doing my head in, trying to do it right – right for you, not so much for me.

By the end of the session with this willing client, the therapist said:

Th.:   You've told me several things that are troubling you, John. There's the internet porn, and not being able to make love to your wife, and this general sense of anxiety. In your own words, you feel out of touch with yourself. And I have been remarking how very in touch with me you have been. So what is your prescription for yourself?

John: I'd leave that to you.

Th.:   What I will leave with you is your decision about continuing counselling with me.

John: It's all right. I know now, I'm happy to go on. If we can set some dates.

Th.:   As I said, give yourself a night to mull over, then ring me tomorrow at lunchtime to say if you still want to continue. And if you do, we can find out more about what you are wanting from coming to see me.

The therapist has put the decision of whether to continue very clearly in the hands of the client, and left him some reflection time before that decision. He has already said that he is 'not quite sure it is worth it' to get in touch with his feelings. Now he can consider at leisure. So she has made clear that he rather than the therapist is in charge of his therapy. She made clear on the phone before they met that the first meeting would give both of them a chance, in her words, to see if they felt they could work together. Assessment was in this way made an overtly two-way process. What is more, she has not spelled out that his worried need to please is to be a focus of their work. He might have agreed, just to please her, rather than because he independently had decided.

Contact as diagnostic

If we look back again at the fragment of conversation between John and the therapist, you will see that she uses her observations and sense of how he behaves towards her and in her presence as a way of beginning to make tentative guesses about his needs from therapy. He did not come into the consulting room worrying overtly about his general way of being with people. He sees himself as beset with anxiety, and as something of a failure towards his wife, and towards himself for resorting to internet porn. What the therapist quickly picked up was what she called his other-centredness, and she commented on it. She spoke of what was obvious here and now, though not in the forefront of John's mind. What he then told of his childhood was of a piece with his sensitivity to her rather than himself. This prompted her to make her clear statement at the end of the session, reiterating her observation about how he put her first. She added a question about what she smilingly termed a prescription he might make for himself. But perhaps the word was misleading, or the idea itself. In any case, he refused, by once more returning to her: 'I leave that to you.' That has left her wanting to return to this next time they meet, if they do.

As well as observing John's way of being with her, the therapist keeps awareness of her own responses. Many schools of counselling lump these together as counter-transference, meaning the particular responses evoked by this person in this setting. In supervision the therapist reported having felt mild alarm during her talk with John, as she guessed how very easy it would be to influence him. He had seemed likely to be an introjector, a swallower-whole of what she might offer. She confessed that she had been surprised to hear herself ask him what he would pre-scribe for himself, as the word prescription did not as a rule come into her mind when she was working. Then she had realised that she was rather desperately trying to return responsibility to the client, or at least to make clear that she was not going to offer solutions to him. The super-visor agreed with her that the word was likely to have alarmed John.

Transparency

Something else to note in their talk is how soon the therapist has described a major method she will be using, that of staying with present awareness and phenomenological dialogue. This method, so familiar to the counsellor, is in all probability completely new to the client. To introduce it without explanation would risk appearing mys-terious and guru-like, if not mildly mad.

In any therapy, there is very likely a power imbalance between the parties, particularly at the beginning. The client feels distress of some kind, and very often feels somewhat shamed or low at having to seek help. So he is likely to want the therapist to be an all-powerful, all-knowing figure who will quickly make his life right. On the other hand, he may so hate being in the position of help-seeker that he finds fault with the therapist and competes with her in a host of ways. Both these attitudes, and the gradations between them, are concerned with estab-lishing a power relationship in which one person is up and the other is down. The gestalt therapist works at establishing a relationship in which both parties are daring to co-operate rather than covertly compete.

Self as function

The word dare may seem surprising here. As was explained more fully in Chapter Two, gestalt notes two ways of being. These are with self as an image, meaning how you appear, or self as function, what you are doing. If you think back to any time when you are fully engaged in what you are doing, you will notice the paradox that by being fully present you are at the same time in some way self-forgetful. Perls saw this as psychological health, to be fully engaged in the moment and all its implications.

With self as image, a person is engrossed in the impression he will make, in how he will come across. Other people's judgement is being put in front of his own. His psychological wellbeing, even survival, seems to him to depend on making the right impression on others, rather than discovering the right thing for him to do.

Here is a paradox at the heart of gestalt theory. The belief is that fully aware responses are inevitably what we can call social rather than individualistic. The phony response, of me doing what I think you would like me to do, and you going along with that rather than say you don't like it, is an extremely common way of behaving, which leaves everyone depleted in energy, excitement and growth. But what I am calling phony, insincere responses may be what a client brings to therapy. It may be a long haul to his finding that becoming what he probably terms selfish or demanding, leads to honest relationship and liveliness.

To return to our first encounter between John and the therapist, the conversation suggests that the therapist had the confidence to be primarily interested in what unfolded between her and John. He seems to have behaved in a servant to master way, or perhaps a patient to doctor way, expecting her to be in charge and give answers and explanations and solutions. In supervision later the therapist said she experienced him as a nervous little animal, approaching, then retreating and asking questions which seemed more fearful than straightforwardly curious. In that same supervision she criticised herself for using the word prescription, saying she had been surprised to hear herself say it. Her supervisor said that it reminded her of the doctor–patient relationship the therapist had imagined to be in John's mind. So the therapist had for a moment melted into, been confluent with, John's sense of the kind of system therapy would be. This was a reminder to the therapist not to take on a doctor role if John returned.

John did return. Most of the second session was taken up with his somewhat agitated account of a row he had just had with his wife, and his terror that she would now leave him. In an ideal world, this session would have been spent in broadening and deepening the awareness of both of them, about the main focus of their coming work together. But this row, in itself, and in his response to it as a symptom of his usual way of being with others, flooded his awareness and needed to be attended to.

By the third session John was calm enough to attend to the process of his awareness, rather than just the content of it. At the back of the therapist's mind was one of Perls' major concepts:

> I believe that ... awareness per se and of itself can be curative. Because with full awareness you become aware of this organismic self-regulation, you can let the organism take over without interfering, without inter-rupting, we can rely on the wisdom of the organism. And the contrast to this is the whole pathology of self-manipulation, environmental control and so on, that interferes with this subtle organismic self-control. (Perls 1969: 17)

Without using these jargon words, John began to see his pathological self-manipulation, his urgent need to make everything right for the other person, at his own expense.

John: But I can see why she was so angry with me, for spending money on therapy when she's the injured party.

Th.:   You can see her point of view.

John: Well, it embarrasses me to spend money...

Th.:   And the end of that sentence?

John: I was going to say, to spend money on myself. And I suddenly remembered that Fran bought two hats last week, for one wed-ding. Quite expensive hats. Only she took against the first one. She spent the same as four sessions with you would cost.

Th.:   That sounds like you arguing your own corner, John. And when you listen to your voice?

John: I sounded a bit indignant, didn't I? There really is something in what you say about me kowtowing the whole time. I need to change that.

Th.: Yes, that way of yours struck me last time as well, as I told you. So shall we agree to keep that in focus as we meet, so you notice all that goes on for you when you do what you call kowtowing?

Later in the session the therapist explained more about her way of working, and set up a regular appointment time for John.

The working alliance

Th.: It's almost time, I notice. And we've settled that we'll concentrate first on how you put other people before yourself. Fritz Perls used to set homework, as he called it, for people coming to him for therapy. The homework was to go over again everything you remember about the session. I suspect that you are doing that already?

John: O yes, I am. And I shall certainly go on...

Th.: [interrupting with a smile] And my heart is sinking. I am being one of the people you have to please.

John: I want to remember. I want to get everything I can out of seeing you.

Th.: O! Already you are contradicting me, and you are saying what you want.

The session ends in laughter.

Emotional process

What has been established is an open agreement between them to focus on what the therapist called John's other-centredness, which could also be termed his lack of assertiveness. The gestalt methods of dialogue and experiment have been explained, so John understands what they are going to do together and how they are going to do it. That understanding can be called the working alliance between them.

It will be greatly influenced, enhanced or even undermined, by the emotional flow between them from session to session. However clear the agreement seems to be about the focus of the therapy, how the two feel about and respond to each other is crucial in the way the work proceeds. It will be at once the diagnostic of how that work is going and of other ways John tends to deal with people. In supervision the therapist is reminded of how important it will be with John to avoid being the expert or master to whom he is subservient, as might have happened at the end of the session just quoted.

Authority and self-responsibility

The therapist is likely to know a good deal more than John about the various theories of human behaviour and motivation. It may be easy for John, as for many clients, to suppose that this knowledge in the therapist means that she will be able to see through him and out the other side. In other words, it will be easy, as we have already seen, for the client to hand all authority and power to the therapist.

What he will be encouraged to notice in gestalt therapy is that he is the world authority on his inner process, on all that goes on in him that is available to his awareness, but that can only be guessed at by anyone else unless he chooses to explain. As the therapist shows acceptance of whatever of this he tells, he will at best come to accept himself as existing as he does. He will little by little lose his judgemental way of experiencing himself. Then he will know his reality, as a creature who is in major ways like most other humans, who eats and breathes, who bleeds if he is cut. In some ways he is unique; but he is not uniquely unworthy or weak or dreadful, as he probably considered himself when he first came to therapy.

All major schools of counselling ultimately work to create such self-confidence in the client. What I describe here is the gestalt way of encouraging this central aspect of any therapeutic experience. The client's responsibility for himself is made clear from the outset.

Dimensions of awareness

Gestalt therapists learn to notice, to let into awareness as much as may be of what is happening in the system created by the two people together in the counselling room. All their senses can be involved in this. They learn that it is not enough to listen to the words the client utters. They are very important, yes, and so is the way of telling. The same words might be muttered or declaimed, blushed over or laughed away, wrenched out in grudging phrases or rattled along so there is no space for reply. The how of what is said tells its own story of the way the client breathes. That in turn says much about how muscles are held, and thus how the skeleton is modified. All this suggests how desirable it is to counsel face-to-face rather than through the internet or telephone, as the new technologies tempt.

As well as what the client tells, then, we have begun to speak of his behaviour in the way he tells it. Not just his manner of speaking but all his behaviour is him in action, him showing his life in relation to the therapist. What he does needs to be a whole dimension of assessment, constantly in the awareness of the therapist.

Gestalt therapy requires attention too to background, to context. Two major parts of any client's context are, first, the difficulty or distress, the apparent need that brought him to therapy. The next, of equal importance, is the whole life that becomes manifest in myriad ways right there in the consulting room. The large field he inhabits is his personal life experience, his culture, place, nation and more. Rather than taking a history, as is the starting point in many schools of psychotherapy, the gestalt counsellor trusts that all the relevant past will in different ways become manifest right there in the present.

Many clients will without prompting tell a good deal about themselves. As well as taking note of what is made clear, the gestalt counsellor sees the possibility of a significant missing element. One person will tirelessly tell of his father, without mentioning his mother at all. Another leaves the wife, with whom he spends every night of his life, out of the therapeutic conversation. In gestalt, value is given to such ways of presenting a life story. Requiring a chronological account would very likely obscure the client's idiosyncratic way of treating the facts of his existence. John was a client who immediately provided some significant facts about himself, about the death of his father when he was eight, his mother's low coping ability, and his having two younger sisters.

Gerda, another client, behaved very differently in her first session. She was 26, bulimic and self-harming, still living with her parents, and had been referred by a psychiatrist. Her mother made the first contact by phone, and when the counsellor asks to speak to Gerda directly, her prospective client has not sounded friendly.

On her first visit, she bangs the door of the consulting room and flops into the chair usually used by the counsellor, and whose glasses and diary lie beside it. The counsellor feels indignant, then a little afraid, so she sits herself in the client chair and sets herself to imagine what is going on for Gerda, who is looking round the room, never at the counsellor. After a pause the counsellor supposes that Gerda would be ready to sit in silence for 50 minutes, so she starts:

Th.: You've got yourself here, with a bit of a bang.

Gerda: I crash about. Everyone tells me.

Th.: So I've behaved just like other people do towards you. And you're saying that you're doing what you always do.

Silence, during which the counsellor notices Gerda's breathing and her own. Gerda's breathing is shallow, with almost no body movement discernible. The therapist herself is breathing deeply and slowly. She has regained her balance, her stability, in this odd scene.

Th.: I'm noticing that our eyes have not met yet.

Gerda: I didn't know that was one of the rules.

Th.: When you said that I found myself imagining a very strict school or something. O, you've looked at me suddenly.

Gerda: I suppose you got that about my boarding school out of the psychiatrist's report.

Th.: I haven't seen a report. I wanted to meet you and hear what you want, rather than start off with someone else's impressions of you.

Gerda: So what have you decided about me then?

Th.: I really winced when you said that. I could imagine rows of professionals handing out judgements on you. You asked what I've decided. But I haven't heard what you want. That is what interests me.

There is silence again.

Gerda: It's never up to me what I want. I don't even know what I want.

Th.: I can believe that. I felt sad hearing it.

Gerda: Well aren't you going to tell me what's good for me?

Th.: No. You'll know that better than I ever can. You're inside you. And you've told me that you're just not in touch with what you want. So finding that could be a focus for us, unless something else comes up for you.

The counsellor suspects that Gerda is likely to fend off anything that sounds like an imposition from her. And she hopes that the words 'unless anything else comes up for you' may spur Gerda into naming a want. This indeed happens, albeit negatively.

Gerda: Well I don't want to be jawed about what's good for me, for a start. Or be sent to bookbinding classes. As if I ever read a book except on line.

Th.: Bookbinding? That doesn't sound like you.

Gerda: You're right. It's not.

Th.: So you really know what you don't want. I notice your energy. [She laughs]

A little later in the same conversation the counsellor goes on:

Th.: I get a picture of you still there with your parents and all sorts of other concerned people. And it sounds as if everyone is stuck, them giving suggestions and you holding on to your independence the only way you can, by refusing everything offered.

It took not just this session but most of several more to reach an agreement on the focus of the work. The counsellor reported in supervision that she guessed things might go more easily than before, when Gerda, without prompting, chose the client chair.

Gerda: You said stuck, and I am stuck. Despair. I'm petrified about leaving home and at the same time I absolutely can't stand being there.

Th.:   It's ghastly, but outside might be even more horrible? I have the image of the door in front of you...

Gerda: [Interrupts] It's stupid, I see other people just getting on with life. But opening that door... [She rolls her eyes] The fear!

Th.:   So do I read you right, that you'd like to get rid of that fear? And be free to lead your own life?

Gerda: You bet.

Th.:   So tell me your fantasy of that life you could lead.

The working alliance is established. She and the counsellor come to understand a picture of some of the hopes Gerda will let herself have.

Fantasy

Perls spoke of the world inside each of us, with its amazing intricacy, its dynamism of cells, organs, nerves, musculature, hormones, electrical impulses and more. Then there is the vast world outside the body, the environment with which we are in constant interaction. Then he named a third area that he called the **maja**. This is the misty system inside all of us, of beliefs, irrationality, fantasy. Some of these may be debilitating, restricting; others sustain hope and ambition and are creativity itself.

Gerda's crippling present fantasy is of some nameless catastrophe if she leaves her parents. Talking to the counsellor, she lets herself notice another, and this time a hopeful, fantasy. She sees herself living in a cottage like her grandmother's, keeping hens and looking after children. Over the next 18 months this fantasy largely came into being for Gerda. She lodged with a family in a village and took a job as an assistant at the local primary school. The bulimia stopped, and the counsellor was told of only one slight self-harming, after a quarrel with one of the teachers. The counsellor had patiently sought Gerda's dream of what she could imagine in her life if she did more than slash at the emotional brambles of all around her that she loathed and yet was caught by.

In gestalt words, she reconfigured the field and saw a new figure, a new and positive foreground. She allowed herself hope, one of the necessary ingredients in any successful therapy.

In supervision the therapist told her own fantasy, of what made Gerda first take her chair for several sessions and then go to the one usually used by clients. She saw it as part of Gerda's desperate holding on to power, for fear of being overpowered. When her supervisor asked what had kept her from talking about this with Gerda, she was not very sure. But she decided that she had been worried that in some way she would have been prolonging the power struggle between them. She had not forgotten the incident but had found it was enough to work at befriending Gerda rather than risk shaming her.

Therapeutic focus

Apparently Fritz Perls was rather like Sherlock Holmes in that he would suddenly tell strangers things about themselves, to their surprise. The secret was that he tirelessly studied behaviour and had the experience to make sound clinical deductions from what he saw. At best, this meant that he could quickly engage clients in a dialogue or experiment that might be uncomfortable but was certainly useful to them.

Modern gestalt counsellors may not always have that experience or acute observation. Some choose to track the client, following where he leads, often reflecting what he says, rather in the same way as person-centred counsellors do. Any important focus in the work is trusted to emerge as they go along. Others spend time in the early sessions, more as described here, coming to an agreement with the client about what they are working on, and how.

The need organises the field. If the client is in touch with what he needs, then the counsellor needs to be aware of that and respect it. Assessment will then be mostly about whether and how the two are going to work together.

Brian came to a counsellor after a clear written statement that he wanted to stop being angry with his partner. Finding how to work with that turned out to have complications.

Th.: You want to stop being angry. And what do you want to do instead?

Brian: I've not come about what I'm to do. It's that Ian's got to stop being so irritating. I don't know how to get it across to him.

Th.: The difficulty for me is that he is not here. He's not my client, and you are.

Brian: I've never met anyone like him. He just doesn't communicate.

Th.: I'm noticing that some of what I say doesn't seem to communicate to you.

Brian: Now you sound like him. Look, are you getting my point or aren't you?

Th.: Brian, I really want to get your point. The real point. I would like you to achieve what you want from coming to see me.

[In supervision the therapist reported that as she said this, she had an unexpected strong suspicion that Brian was frightened that his partner was going to leave him]

Brian: [In a more subdued tone] If he'd just listen to me.

Th.: [Gently] I have not felt that you have listened to me very much. And I find I'm tensing all through my centre. It's a strange pent-up feeling that I wonder if I've picked up from you. In my fantasy it adds up to something like 'when there's so much pain inside me, how can I listen to anyone else?'

Brian: That's nonsense.

Th.: You've gone very pale. And it sounds as if my words connected, from the speed with which you replied.

Brian: I'm really not sure if this is what I want. Is it going to do any good?

Th.: It takes two to tango. I think it will take both of us to do any good.

Brian: [After a pause] I suppose I don't listen to him either.

Th.: And I notice you are listening to me now. You're still very white. Do you listen to yourself? Take notice of what you need?

Brian: When you say that, I think I do nothing but try and educate, not educate, train him up. He's the whole focus.

Brian's manner has softened and the therapist notices that she has relaxed. She listens as Brian remembers a childhood where his hated stepfather behaved just as he now sees himself behaving to Ian. By staying with the information in the room, with Brian's words, and his and her bodily reactions, the pair move with apparent speed to a direction in their work together. The therapist's ability to hear Brian's almost contemptuous irritation, and comment interestedly on aspects of it rather than retaliate, seems to have inspired his trust.

What the task is can generally in gestalt be discovered by the therapist's attention to the **contact-boundary**, the way the two meet and interact, as well as the story the client brings, important though that is. How that task is undertaken will be massively influenced by their attitude, their opinion and feelings towards each other. The gestalt therapist keeps in the field, as an element in her gestalt formation, **the underlying distress that has brought the client to her room**, no matter the behaviour he brings as well.

The vignettes of assessment sessions here demonstrate one of the major methods in gestalt therapy phenomenological dialogue. This valuable art, very simple, but unusual to adhere to, is the subject of the next chapter.

Experiment

Observe or Interpret

In everyday life we often observe and interpret almost at the same time. This can be very useful, unless the difference between the two is confused. This exercise is to remind you of the observing stance used by gestalt therapists. Next time you are watching a waitress in a cafe, or a child playing, tell yourself silently all you are noticing, all the demonstrable evidence you have about the person from what you see and hear or take in through other senses. Then notice what you are experiencing as the observer. How are you standing or sitting? How is your breathing and heart rate? The degree of tension in your muscles?

As you do this, you are likely to add, 'Ah yes, that's because...'. Notice these little interruptions of interpreting, and see if you return to the observing or enter into an inner dialogue of self-blame, about whether you are bad at doing the exercise, perhaps, or blame, deciding that the exercise is boring or uninformative. In doing all this, you will be finding out more about your capacity to observe interactively, both the other and yourself by turns.

FOUR

Gestalt Dialogue

A major method in gestalt suffers from the unfortunately long-winded name phenomenological dialogue. In the vignettes in the last chapter some of what was quoted was an example of this.

Even before beginning an explanation of this unfortunate phrase, it may be useful to look searchingly at some of the ways we use and construct language. Persona, or person, is a word made up of two Latin ones: *per* means through, and *sona* means sounds. This is a startling statement, a long way from Descartes' cogito ergo sum. It is saying that we are somehow registering ourselves here in the world through our sounds, our speech. Speech is a major way of communicating with each other. The self is forged in interaction. So our personhood is involved with, at least partly dependent on, speech, in this communicating called contact in gestalt theory. Erving Polster stressed this contactful task: 'The first step, therefore, is for the therapist himself to meet the patient in a face to face encounter where authenticity of expression and communication are primary' (Stephenson 1975: 156).

English is very rich, arguably better at describing outer reality than in capturing in everyday language the nuances of perception, the how of experiencing. So the early gestaltists paid great attention to what people said, as well as how they did it. They relentlessly pointed out the habitual ways clients, like most of us much of the time, distort meaning.

They pointed out, for example, how common it is to muddle pronouns, and so to muddle meanings. 'You have to have a big car, don't you?' is unlikely to be a comment on someone else's obligations. It sounds like a more complicated statement about the speaker's need for status. One and you and everybody and people are frequent cyphers for I, and can serve to disguise even to the speaker the nub of what she is talking about.

Here are some examples I have heard from clients in therapy. A middle-aged man said rather crossly, 'Nobody remembers their childhood.' It took many sessions before he saw that he had striven to forget his own bewildering early years. He said later that he felt as if he had drawn a black curtain over his early memories, and his way of keeping it drawn was to make believe that everyone did the same. As it turned out, when he let himself remember he discovered a rich and rewarding personal history, alongside some sad events he had tried rather unsuccessfully to deny.

A young woman assured me, on her first visit, that people are really really stupid. I said that she and I were people, so it seemed as if in her estimation we must be stupid too. This upset her. She said she had looked me up and knew my qualifications, and I replied that I knew many people with all sorts of letters after their names who could behave very stupidly, as I could. By this time I had noticed that I was in a verbal jousting match with her, so I named this, adding that I felt wrong and a bit fearful as I produced my smart answers. By and by we discovered between us that she spent a lot of time in what I had called verbal jousting. What lay under it was a dread that she would be seen to be stupid. She habitually projected stupidity on to the world, rather than allow into awareness the possibility that it might belong to her.

English lets us muddle meaning when talking about perception. 'You made me forget...' is something we have all said or heard, and probably believed. How could it be my fault that I forgot to put the cat out, when you had called to me to look at a shooting star? The awkward truth is that I am the one who forgot. I did it, or rather, did not do it. It is convenient to say it was your fault; but the actuality is different. What happened is that I went into the kitchen to get the cat, you called, so I went back and stargazed, and then went to bed. I did all those things, choosing to go straight back when you called, choosing then to go to bed. It is an inconvenient truth that I am the person who performs my actions, and so am responsible for them.

'Happiness just swept over me' is another common grammatical form in English. It makes happiness, or whatever emotion is being discussed, seem to be an outside force, swooping on its hapless victim whenever it wants to. A sudden burst of feeling is certainly easily described in that way, in this language at least. Other languages express things differently. In French, for example, there are reflexive verbs that show the retroflection in such a statement. This would translate as 'I make myself happy, or sad or whatever else'. This is a very different, and an accurate, construct. It clearly makes the speaker responsible for her feeling.

The verb to feel is itself one that we use to mislead ourselves in English. It is clear enough that it means 'I am experiencing this or that emotion'. It is an intransitive verb that does not travel from the speaker to another object, like such transitive verbs as 'I hit', or 'I stroke'. These need an object, a something or someone hit or stroked, for the hearer to make sense of what is said. What I feel, by contrast, is what I feel, and that is that. However, most of us are inclined to bend it to mean something else, as in 'I feel that you are not doing your best today'. Here the word feel is used where guess or judge or suppose would be more accurate. Gestalt therapists are trained to be careful to use words accurately, as they realise how much inaccurate language reflects or even brings about inaccurate perception.

A confusion between what can be observed and what is more a matter of opinion has come into English. I see someone sitting with his elbows on his desk, red-faced, heaving a great sigh. I may look at him and say 'What's made you angry, then?'

He replies, 'What do you mean?' I then point out the evidence. And he tells me that he is simply puffed: the lift is broken, he has just walked up four floors and is trying to get his breath back. I have accused him of what he is feeling, which is something I cannot know for certain. All I could really be sure of were the physical signs I noticed, that turned out to have a different meaning altogether in that case.

I can notice that someone is slurring his words, but that alone does not mean that he is drunk. My former literary agent, a teetotaller, had lunch in a hotel in New York and in the lobby did indeed stagger and become inarticulate. A frightened clerk sent for the police, who took him to the drunk tank, a horrible place where within two hours he died of the brain haemorrhage he was suffering. This tragedy is an extreme reminder of the importance of separating data from over-quick conclusions about their meaning.

Reification

In Latin this word is made of *res*, meaning thing, and *facere*, meaning make. In English it is easy to make thing-words, nouns, to talk about what we really experience as dynamic, shifting, living. A client said, 'I have difficulties with the atmosphere at my workplace.' This was a sentence with several thing-words. I asked what he was experiencing as he spoke. He replied that the coldness in the place was mentioned by other employees, so it was really something about the place rather than him. I asked more about his own sensations. After a moment he said, 'Like going cold where my diaphragm should be.' Soon he described a particular incident in which his female manager had looked up at him as he passed, flared her nostrils and looked away, not smiling. Both of us could make more sense of this series of actions, generated by people, than of the abstract statement about the atmosphere.

The client's recurrent feeling of dread as he walked past his boss's desk was partly evoked in him again as he remembered it, far more than when he converted that memory into the word atmosphere. Abstract nouns like atmosphere are often useful. And they are sometimes used, as here, to stave off reality.

Neuroscience has shown how we constantly enact, at some minute or larger level, whatever we are thinking or talking about. Perls pre-empted that observation, saying that we are always in action, and that we just live more or less intensely. He believed that the energy generated by each figure, or foreground, of a gestalt needs to be translated into action in the world. So with this client we discovered a cascade of actions could follow from what he remembered and described concretely. Over the next weeks he discovered how his dread of the boss was a re-evoking of his dread of seeing his mother unsmiling and looking away when his father had been sent to prison and there was no money for more than essentials. He went through a great deal of re-experiencing and finishing what was unfinished within himself. In the world, he plucked up courage to speak to the boss about her grim face. She was relieved to talk. He discovered that the firm was under threat from litigation. In a strange way, financial ruin haunted her as it had his mother.

The early gestaltists cultivated a keen awareness of how people talk, and were fascinated with how that affected, or was intended to affect, the person listening. Speech is interactive, intersubjective. It is not just one person's expression, it is potentially a very rich way of contacting others. A very quiet voice, for example, might sometimes camouflage a huge need for power, making the other person strain and hold their breath to follow what is being said. The myriad styles of talking that people invent all say something about those people's context, their history, their attitude to the person addressed, and perhaps as much about unresolved parts of their lives. Perls alleged that clients in therapy tirelessly re-present their major conflicts every 30 seconds or so. This may be through little patterns of other behaviour, but is likely too to be through their whole manner of talking.

Phenomenology

'What a beautiful sunset.' As you read this statement, you probably give it a setting, and vaguely imagine a red sky, or some place where you often see sunsets. You may go further and put a voice to the words. In one mood, you may imagine the words being spoken grandly, by someone apparently wanting to be appreciated as sensitive and artistic. In another mood, you perhaps have a lift of the heart, and hear a young and eager voice seeming to love what he sees and almost be lost in it. Your heart rate may change a little as you imagine whatever interpretation you put on this little statement. Even the words on the page undoubtedly evoke an organismic response in you, a physical echo of looking at a sunset. For the purposes of therapy rather than philosophy, it is this unique response, probably different in each one of us on every occasion, that phenomenology seeks to express. So, at its simplest, if I manage to convey what I can of the impact on me of my present experience, I have made a phenomenological statement.

In dialogue, my present experience is very likely to be concerned with you. So, if two of us are watching this sunset, it may be that some of what I have to say, if I really notice what is going on, is: 'I feel the whole of my body relax as I see that amazing sky, and I realise that I want you to feel as awestruck and released as I do. I want to give you what is there for me in this sight.' That sounds a close, even a loving statement.

Or it might be that I respond: 'I suddenly breathe deeper as I look at that sky, and I realise how tense and bored I was getting, listening to you. I want some quiet.' This equally truthful statement is likely to provoke a very different reply than if I had stayed with the external statement, 'What a beautiful sunset.' Socially most of us shorthand many of our statements, from many motives. A gestalt therapist searches for a more accurate brief statement, if that is possible.

Whatever happens in and round us registers constantly in our bodies. Neuroscience shows us this factually. Perception is body response, and it is the centre of gestalt psychology and hence therapy. Gestalt therapy theory suggests that experience first registers as sensation, an impact on sight, hearing, touch, smell or proprioception, an inward jolt. So, in phenomenological dialogue, the task is to register this sensation and its flowering into a feeling, an impulse, a memory or image, and then find the words to convey this process. This is a long way from most social conversation.

Phenomenological dialogue

In its root meaning in Greek, dialogue means talking through, or talking thoroughly. Phenomenon is a comparatively common word in English, and is a fancy way of naming a happening. So, in a pure co-operative use of this unusual and therapeutically valuable form of conversation, the parties to it talk in depth, thoroughly. And importantly, they do so by reporting the internal, the intrapsychic happenings that occur to them from moment to moment.

This way of talking was invented by those philosophers who understood how inadequate it is for humans to say they can be objective, removing their own values and prejudices from whatever they are discussing. Instead, the phenomenologists introduced an intensely personal, subjective way of conversing, in which each speaker reported the phenomena, the fragments of sensation, feeling, memory, image or whatever that came to him on hearing what the other said. In this way, the hope was to progress towards the kernel, the subjective heart of each person's truth.

Therapeutic phenomenological dialogue

These philosophers would be talking in the field of philosophical enquiry, a no-holds-barred dredging of their perceptions and ideation. When therapists use this method, they do so in the field of therapy. The client and her life, so far as they know it, frame the field of dialogue. This difference of context makes for a difference of perception. In an everyday example, if I am just finishing work and someone suggests hurrying to the cinema to catch the early showing of a new film, I may well agree enthusiastically, without a moment's doubt. But if I am looking after two toddlers when that person phones with the same idea, I either feel aggrieved and indignant at her ignoring what I am doing, or I need to go straight into urgent problem-solving mode, to find other care for the children. The context or field in which I hear this suggestion hugely affects how I respond to it.

In just the same way, when in the therapy room, the therapist knows where she is and who she is with. That perception will change the field for her. A later section in this chapter, on bracketing, says more about this.

Let us look here at this simple, yet unusual, way of talking that we call phenomenological dialogue. An ordinary social exchange might go like this:

A: Hi, how are you?

B: Fine. By the way, do you happen to have brought that book back?

A: Well I really meant to, but I had to get Emily to play school. Tomorrow?

If we unpack this into the real responses between these two people, the conversation might be:

A: Ow, I'm scared. My heart rate has gone up and I'm imagining how angry you would be if you knew Emily has scribbled all over that book.

B: I can feel my jaw setting. I'm irritated at your big smile, and you asking how I am. I want to shake you for keeping that book for three weeks, when I need it for my essay. And I'm scared you won't like me if I say that.

A: Now I'm blushing, and I'd like to fall through the floor. Maybe I can get to a bookshop before tomorrow? No, that's a really expensive book. I'm so scared at how you'll feel about me if I tell you what happened.

Even this lengthy translation will not contain all the responses going on between these two students in this brief exchange. There is perhaps enough here to give a sense of the elements of this sort of dialogue. The speakers report what they feel and or sense, or even do. They report the memories and fantasies, imaginings, wants, that are generated by the meeting. Some gestalt therapists work precisely like this, offering their own responses to whatever the client says. So if A was the client and came in with the same greeting: 'Hi, how are you?' The therapist might respond:

Th.:   I felt a sort of frisson, a slight unease through my heart, as you spoke. Now what's that about? I think I was struggling with different responses. One was almost alarm, that you have paid me to raise awareness about how you are, and now you have turned the tables on me. As I say that I feel that alarm more, as if there is a power battle between us. And another response is warmth, a gratefulness that you might care about me.'

This is a long and careful reply. It is all about the present. The client might then say:

> A: I've had a terrible week.

Perhaps, if she knew A well, the therapist would say,

> Th.:   Now I felt something like cloth tearing inside me. I felt a spurt of anger. You speak as if I had not said anything.

Then A might say:

> A: O, I heard you. But I've had a terrible week, and you said it yourself, this is my therapy, not yours.
>
> Th.:   The image comes to me of being pushed out of the way.
>
> A: Well tell me what I'm supposed to do to make you happy.
>
> Th.:   I felt a pang of sadness when I heard the words 'make you happy'. I'm imagining that you are unhappy. Very unhappy.

In a session where a conversation very like this happened, the client then wept. Over the next half hour she began to see how her terrible week had been to do with snubbing and keeping out the very people she wanted to confide in, as she had just done to the therapist.

In phenomenological dialogue, the therapist always responds with what is present for her. The client is at the forefront of her awareness, so most of what the therapist senses, feels and imagines is directly to do with the system the two of them form. It is not her job to make the client do the same.

Perls said that it was the work of the therapist to keep the client in the present, and to frustrate his every effort to escape from the present. This is what inevitably happens in this form of dialogue. The present is returned to, or rather it is as fully acknowledged as may be, every time the therapist speaks. In that sense, the client cannot escape from it.

Gestalt is a process therapy, examining carefully how the client perceives, how he interacts, how he maintains his self-esteem or undermines it. His effect on another person is often a huge clue to all this, so by revealing her own responses the therapist is raising the client's awareness of his effect on at least one other person. It is unlikely that the therapist's responses will be unlike those of many others, but this too will be talked over.

The talking over may be almost tutorial at times. James Simkin was an early advocate of the use of phenomenological dialogue in therapy, and in his training film quoted in Stephenson (1975: 11) he explains as well as enacts this way of talking. He is showing the client how to be present, so that he is better able to feel the excitement, novelty and fullness that is potential in so many moments of life.

The example of dialogue in the section above was completely reciprocal, in the sense that the therapist reported the phenomena entering her awareness as the client spoke. She used statements rather than asking questions.

Focused dialogue

Many gestalt therapists use questions in order to focus the client's mind on their present experience. So, when A said he had had a terrible week, she might have said,

Th.:   What are you feeling as you say that?

A: Well I'm sorry for myself. Wouldn't you be?

Th.:   Where in your body do you register that feeling?

A: O, everywhere. I just wish you'd listen to me.

Th.:   I am not sure that you are listening to yourself. I want you to notice how you sound.

A: I sound impatient because I am impatient.

What the therapist does here is concentrate on the client and his phenomena, his internal or intrapsychic experience. She does this by questions, and by the request 'I want you to....'.

This is a qualitatively different form of phenomenological dialogue from the first one illustrated. At best it will let the client discover himself more. At worst it can become an interrogation which gives the official power to the therapist, leaving the client to try and take power by whatever, possibly devious, means he can devise. Perls described inner conflicts as often having sides which were top dog and under dog. The top dog, rather like the superego, might in this questioning form of dialogue seem to lodge in the therapist. But as Perls pointed out, in all such tussles the under dog usually wins, by non-co-operation, playing dumb or other creative means. So the risk here is that A takes on the under dog role, as he is beginning to here, with his false co-operation: 'I sound impatient because I am impatient.'

At this point the therapist needs to broaden the focus from the client's registering of sensation and feeling to his intersubjective response, his feelings and wants towards the therapist. This may be more uncomfortable for the therapist than her interrogation technique.

All psychotherapy is sociotherapy, as Freud himself said. Other people are inextricably involved with us. In the dialogue consisting mostly of disclosing statements by both people, the intersubjective, the response of each to other, is revealed from the beginning. In the focused, questioning style, if the therapist is trusted, the client who is very out of touch with himself will be able to discover vital clues he is suppressing in himself, in terms of his sensations and feelings, as they are indicated by body movements, his voice and breathing.

Power and intimacy in dialogue

Sonia Nevis (2003) highlights these two facets of family life. They are relevant too in the smaller setting of individual therapy. Between people, the word power can sound threatening. It may suggest that one person is going to have the power, to win, to disempower the other.

Energy and power are interchangeable words in some contexts. We talk of electricity as the energy supply or the power supply. If the word energy is used, it makes it obvious that unless all parties galvanise some energy, there will be a dull encounter. But power is a powerful idea. It can lead to survival fears. All therapy needs to respect the client so that he does not need to feel his power, which is his authority and sense of himself, to be under threat. In other words, the therapist aims to be comfortable enough in her own skin to have a sense of herself and her authority, without having to become just a role, a sort of schoolteacher, at the expense of her client. John Frew (1992) suggested that there are only three kinds of therapeutic intervention. They are **affirming**, **contesting** or **imposing**. The first two can occur in phenomenological dialogue. The third may be used with the client's consent in experiments, as the next chapter describes. As Carl Rogers believed, affirming responses are often the most therapeutically useful and rewarding. And a number of contesting responses can be seen in the case vignettes I quote.

At best there is a depth of intimacy in the conversation in the therapy room. This inevitably happens if the therapist at least is, from her awareness of the scene she is in, reporting the phenomena that rise to her awareness. The scene is therapy. She is sitting with someone who has come to her in some level of discomfort or distress, and she is there with a role and a task. As the short extracts above show, she may be left for a time to be the only one telling her experience as it happens. This one-sided phenomenological dialogue exposes the client to a sense of this reflective and unthreatening form of conversation.

In psychoanalytic psychotherapy the therapist used to use this method of self-reporting, but without asking the client to do the same. The clients were asked to free associate, which is to say without censoring whatever came into their heads. Perls suggested that rather than free association – the term used to describe this method – it might better be called free disassociation. He asked something different; he asked clients to report phenomena, which is – as we have said – what they experienced from moment to moment. Doing this with new clients gives them a major tool to self and relational awareness. When they understand the task, very many clients attempt at least to do as the therapist does. The ways in which they do otherwise are likely to give insight into how they habitually avoid contact. Then the therapist is free to comment on what she sees happening, in her phenomenological responses. It is her business to comment on the process, not to manage the client's behaviour or lead him to what she thinks is health or anything else. The values and meaning the client gives to his existence are respected by the gestalt therapist.

Bracketing

Field theory is a central gestalt idea, describing how we constantly create dynamic, moving patterns of data relevant to us, from the myriad that are available from moment to moment. It means that when I or you are working as a therapist, we create a field of perception which includes the client, with all that we know or seek to know about him, all the ways that we respond towards him. If we have just been invited to a film, we have said no if that would clash with his appointment. We are in a clear contractual relationship to the client and his time with us. But the word bracketing has come into psychotherapy, so it is not unusual to hear therapists say that they had to bracket off this or that, perhaps this very invitation, in the interests of their work.

What is overlooked here is the gestalt belief in the ability of all of us, of our organisms, to deal with all the data in the field, in terms of the context from which we are indivisible. As soon as the intellect steps in and decides what ought or ought not to be relevant, the organismic process of gestalt formation – an out of awareness bringing to the front the most important figure – has been sidelined. Gestalt formation implies the wisdom of the organism described in the last chapter, an inner configuration of the field that will bring into awareness, make figural, whatever needs to be at the forefront of awareness and acted upon at that moment.

But perhaps a therapist has a raging toothache. How can that be kept in the background except by an aware effort? Most of us have experienced or witnessed the changing or tuning out of one strong experience when another is made figure. A friend went into labour just after seeing her husband off on a long train journey. This meant that he could not be back for 14 hours. The midwife reported that my friend had stuck herself in one stage of labour, and asked if she was waiting for her husband to return, as she knew the couple had been determined to be together for the birth. She was not aware of doing so, and was aware of how nasty it was to be stuck in strong labour. However, the baby appeared 20 minutes after the husband was back. This is a dramatic example of the whole person, the whole organism, evidently controlling events in response to context. Less dramatically, many of us have suddenly realised that we have tuned out a headache in the face of some minor urgency that needed us to act. There are states and happenings that intrude on the therapist when she is working. They are best dealt with by action in the world, not by repressing whatever brought them to awareness. This may on occasion mean cancelling a session or possibly in some circumstances, confessing the headache to the client.

As many gestalt therapists know, speech is often enough action to deal with the intruding thought or feeling. On occasion it turns out to be more connected to the therapy than expected. A supervisee reported that she kept wanting to call her client Jim, though his name was John. She added that she had to bracket this urge. It was suggested that she tell the client, who, when she did, confessed that he was called Jim, his first name, when he was a child. The revelation led to many discoveries about all he had rejected along with his childhood name. This strange perception is of a kind common enough in therapy to warrant being quoted here. Many so-called bracketed perceptions that are reported in supervision are of a more commonplace kind. Another counsellor confessed that she nearly fell asleep in the presence of one client, so she had resorted to pinching herself to stay alert. Prompted by the supervisor, she told the client next time she felt herself glazing over. He was immensely and unexpectedly angry. The counsellor said later to the supervisor that she felt as if a brooding storm had broken and refreshed the whole landscape. She and the client had been in the brooding and uneasy calm that precedes such a storm.

Every school of therapy has its own way of managing the conversation between therapist and client. What I have described here is an engaged meeting of two people in which the therapist offers her authentic present responses, her phenomenology. It is an exposing style, relational and to a great extent on one level, rather than being between expert and uninitiated.

Everyone is the only authority on his or her own experience. In this form of dialogue the client can come to acknowledge actuality, the changing present, finally purged of other people's ideas of what should or should not be.

Experiments

Precision

Next time you are about to utter a general statement to someone, telling them they are such a kind, or clever, or idiotic person, also, or instead, tell them the observations that led to your saying what you did. Generalities are mostly inaccurate. Reporting data is often more informative.

Dialogue

Sit with a partner and use phenomenological dialogue to see what new discoveries you make about yourselves and each other. Ten minutes is a possible time for this experiment. Then take a few minutes more to tell any difficulties you had, and whether you can deal with them.

FIVE

Excitement, Anxiety and Experiment

… fantasy … on the one hand is a drama to try out and become expert, on the other, a therapy to become friendly with the strange and bitter actuality … (PHG 1951: 302)

The subtitle of Perls, Hefferline and Goodman's major work, *Gestalt Therapy* (1951), contains the words 'Excitement and Growth', and the word excitement is in this chapter heading.

Another word here is anxiety. One definition of anxiety is excitement without the action. In other words, anxiety occurs when signals from outside and inside the body are at least partly ignored. This simple description does not dismiss the many other theories of the causes of anxiety. It says what happens when there is heightened excitement, from whatever source; there is an upsurge in metabolic process, but a blocking of the action that would properly fulfil that excitement. One of the ways of translating anxiety into action is through what in this therapy are called experiments, right there in the consulting room. They involve imagining and possibly doing something, rather than only talking about it.

A word about how we experience may be useful here. In gestalt therapy there is recognition that we are all experiencing, all the time. Much of this experience is out of awareness and may usefully stay that way. Some is just in awareness, glimpsed in memories or fantasy; neurobiology can now show us that even such slight phenomena are always bodily experiences, causing changes in body chemistry, even in muscle tone. Even dreams produce minute enactments, or sketches of enactments, of the actions being dreamed about. This is another reminder of the gestalt dictum that mind and body are not separable.

Whether with people or at work alone, most people recognise that there are many levels of intensity in how we experience. We can be fully engaged, excited to the point of being self-forgetful. Or experience can be nearer water off a duck's back, neither wholehearted nor well remembered. Gestalt experiments take the experimenter into action, enactment, and so set up the possibility of learning, by moving towards intensity of experience.

You will see that the third word of the chapter heading is that very one, experiment. The gestalt therapy use of experiments is illustrated first in one of the two books that constitute Perls, Hefferline and Goodman (1951). It is a record of a piece of qualitative research. It is an account of many experiments set by the writers, and undertaken and reported on by students.

The word experiment is usually associated with science, and the project was a novel and in part a deliberate move to give scientific validity to psychological theory. Experiment can be defined as 'an act or operation made to discover some unknown principle or effect, or to test, establish, illustrate, confirm or disprove some suggested or known truth'. This principle underlies the experiments that continue to be part of gestalt therapy for many practitioners, and are indeed much of what supports, extends, and always arises from the phenomenological dialogue we have described already. This chapter will describe some of the kinds and methods used.

A life of experiment

In one sense very many acts in everyday life are experiments. They are chosen actions from which we can learn and develop. If I go to a theatre for the first time, I may discover an exciting world of dramatic art, and learn that the experiment is worth repeating. Or I may find the windowless theatre and serried rows of seats so disquieting that

I decide never to go again. What I have done can be described as an experiment, a chosen action, with a result, from which, as in school science lessons, I can draw a conclusion or learning. A useful experiment is one in which the result is not known until it happens. If I have decided before I go to the theatre that I am going to feel claustrophobic there, the visit is not an experiment, it is a confirmation of my suspicion or prejudice. Good science, then, involves an open-mindedness about how an experiment will develop. And, very importantly, it involves the final stage, the conclusion, or learning from what has happened.

Experiments are used in this therapy for several purposes. One is **to bring novelty and even surprise into the work**. Staying in one mode such as dialogue may after a time lead to lack of attention. This idea of variety of mode is perhaps over-recognised by television companies, with their frequent switches between topics and advertisements. It is better used by any good teacher, and is formally incorporated in one educational system at least. So, just at this level, experiments make a change of rhythm and impact for the client. Another function of experiments is, as already said, **to intensify the experience** of what is being remembered or imagined. Another is to **bring into awareness what is at that time not in the awareness of the client or, indeed, of client and therapist**. Yet another is to **rehearse an unfamiliar but desired social skill.**

Here is an experiment that markedly changed the rhythm and impact of the session in which it happened. John came to his first therapy appointment because his partner had threatened to leave him if he did not change. He banged the door as he came in, and tipped his chair back so that it creaked.

John: No, I like people, I really do. It's just that I'm a bit slapdash.

Th.:   Yes. I've just seen the footmarks you've made across the carpet.

John: [laughs] That's me! Absolutely typical. [He looks at one muddy shoe with apparent interest]

Th.:   I suspect I'm near feeling some of the things you said your partner does when you forget, or break something.

John: Lucky that you're a therapist, then, so I suppose you just have to grin and bear it.

Th.:   What I want to do is make sense of what is going on between us.

John: Surely you've got a cleaner or someone. I'm here for therapy. I'm not interested in talking about a bit of mud on a carpet.

Th.:   What is staying with me is not just the mud on the carpet, but its effect on you. And that phrase, 'grin and bear it', is echoing still for me.

John: Set your mind at rest, lady. The mud had no effect on me whatsoever.

Th.:   [Slowly] I am not surprised that you say that. John, my guess is that you would like me to have no effect on you whatsoever. Even though when we talked about it, you said you were here for yourself, and not just because your partner made a threat.

John: [Vehemently] I want you to have an effect on me! All right, I admit I can be a bit difficult, but I'd like to get out of this glass box I live in. I want you to get me out of it. I want some results.

Th.:   Are you willing to try an experiment, with me suggesting things for you to do?

John: Whatever. Yes.

Th.:   Shut your eyes, yes, like that. Now in your own time bring back that image of the glass box. [Pause] Without talking, just notice what size it is. Feel what it's like inside there. [Pause] Now see if you want to change the size of it in any way. Then do that. [She notices John's breathing relax]. I suggest we stop there. When you're ready, open your eyes and let's talk about what went on.

John: Well, I made it a bit bigger.

Th.:   You had some control over it.

John: It isn't rubbish, you know, that glass box. Nothing really gets to me through it.

Th.:   I have a very different sense of you now. I've relaxed.

John: You got me interested.

A warmer and more co-operative conversation followed.

The therapist reported in supervision that the experiment, so near the beginning, was a gamble on her part, as she sensed the client's extreme impatience. His demand for results was the prompt she followed. As well as this, she was aware of the stonewalling style of conversation at which John seemed disastrously adept.

Her supervisor was curious about what made her stop the experiment when she did. She said she was afraid that if they continued, the client might revert to his default mode of arguing and dismissing. The supervisor pointed out that instead of allowing the client's need for control, the therapist had competed with him. She warned against continuing a covert control battle. For many sessions after that there were no experiments but instead long dialogue, in which the client remembered the events that led to his constructing his glass box, and in which he began to listen, and let in the person talking to him.

Here is another experiment that came about in the first session with Gwen. It is an example of intensifying an experience.

Gwen speaks hesitantly, looking at the floor rather than the therapist.

Gwen: I've always been told that – I just float. I've hardly got my feet on the ground.

Th.: [Smiles] And there's just the toe of one of your shoes on the ground now.

[The client tucks her feet further back under her chair and blushes]

Gwen: Sorry.

Th.: When we know each other better, you'll see that I'm interested in what we both do here, as well as what we say. You just told me something that was clearly true.

Gwen: But I didn't mean not having my feet on the ground literally.

Th.: I understand. And yet you really are hardly touching the ground even now. Literally.

Gwen: Is this more what I should do? [She slowly brings her feet forward and puts them flat]

Th.: Tell me what happens in your body now you are sitting differently.

Gwen: Well, my tummy lets go a bit.

Th.: And I notice that you are using the chair more, leaning on the back.

Gwen: What I really came to see you about was how to be more decisive. [As she speaks she reverts to sitting forward with her feet tucked awkwardly away]

Th.: I'm imagining a sort of Decisiveness Scale, from 1 to 10.

Gwen: Well, if I was filling one in, I'd score about 3. I have managed to tell you what I want, after all.

Th.: And I'm seeing how you've changed your position.

Gwen: I hadn't noticed. [Pause. The client blushes again and then puts her feet forward]

Th.: You want to be more decisive?

Gwen: Sitting this way, I've moved up to 5 or 6. Better.

Th.: So just the way you sit actually changes the way you feel. You've discovered that, and I've discovered that you did not notice when you went back to sitting in a way that looked uncomfortable.

This experiment has let the client see how she enacts and reinforces her sense of herself in her body posture, and how she can change that. It has brought into awareness what the other could see, but she did not notice. The dialogue over later sessions lets her remember the family attitudes leading to her sense of unworthiness or shame, and then evolve from them. This experiment was about only one, albeit important, aspect of her shyness. This was the physical habit that perpetuated her emotional discomfort.

Sometimes an experiment leads to a surprise discovery for both therapist and client.

Ian had been seeing a counsellor for several months, after the early death of his wife. As the summer approached, he reported enormous unease whenever he smelt or saw roses. He felt that this was somehow to do with Dorothy, his wife, but what it was he did not know. He remembered that she liked roses, but that did not account in his mind for the extreme agitation he increasingly felt when near them, to such a point that he was avoiding going into his garden.

Ian:	You talk about unfinished gestalts, I remember. As if there's something – if only I could fish it out of my memory.
Th.:	We could experiment if you would like that.
Ian:	Please.
Th.:	You've connected all this with Dorothy. So if you imagine her sitting on the empty chair near you, see what you need to say to her.
Ian:	[After a pause] I feel I'm letting you down. [Pause] And you've really upset me. I could feel quite annoyed with you.
Th.:	You've clenched your teeth.
Ian:	I am annoyed with you. [He breaks off and turns to the counsellor] This is stupid. Of course I'm not annoyed with her, she's not even here.
Th.:	So you can criticise yourself for what you are saying, or you can listen to yourself. Your choice.
Ian:	Trust the process, as you've taught me. OK. I am annoyed with you, and really agitated, and it's to do with rose – [He stops speaking for a second, then turns to the therapist] O my God, it's Rose. They were best friends at school, and now I absolutely remember a year ago Dorothy and I were at a garden centre, and the rose bushes reminded her of Rose's name, and she said to me that if ever she was run over, would I be sure to tell Rose how much Dorothy valued her. Rose had gone to Australia, you see, so they were quite out of touch. And I got angry. I couldn't bear her talking of dying. That's what put it out of my mind, I'll bet. I'll phone her tonight. I've never given her a thought since Dorothy died.
Th.:	It looks as if you've given her a lot of attention and emotion, Ian.

Very often this device, on the face of it so peculiar, of imagining a person or thing to be in the room and in sight of the client, rather than simply lodged in his mind, suddenly sheds more light and reveals a meaning that was until then missing.

One aim the therapist has is to alert the client to inventing his own experiments, so the creativity of both people informs a session. This important principle is mentioned here, as it might otherwise seem that the therapist has an exclusive role in this part of the work.

Here is an account of a simple experiment that could be said to be co-created, made by both. It is at the beginning of a session, some months into a therapy with someone with difficulty taking responsibility for herself:

Client: I feel very low today, not even wanting to think, somehow.

Th.: And you are bending over, with your head down.

Client: Well that's how I feel.

Th.: So your mood and your body are all of a piece.

Client: You're telling me that if I change how I sit, I'll be out of touch with my low feelings.

Th.: Those are your words.

Client: [Stands up abruptly] All right. See? And now I feel really irritated.

Th.: [Smiles] Let me register this. You've stood up, and you are after all in touch with your feelings, though you predicted you would not be.

Client: But I'm not in touch with my low feelings.

Th.: You already showed me how you can be in touch with them. [There is a pause, during which the client sits, this time leaning back and staring away from the therapist] So you have not gone back to sitting with your head down.

This client has undertaken an experiment, by standing, and discovering, as did Gwen in the experiment described earlier, that her stance does much to generate or reinforce her feelings. Later, in supervision, the therapist said that she had a strong sense that the client, who still lived with her mother at the age of 26, was showing the therapist her way of making her mother feel bad. When she said she felt low, the therapist had a moment of anxiety and self-blame, asking herself if the client's feelings were her fault. Then she remembered the client's many stories of how her mother did not understand her, and did things wrong. So she commented on the client's responsibility for her feelings, rather than commenting on the mood itself, as she might have done with a different person.

When a client has become used to the methods used by many gestalt therapists, he may propose experiments for himself. Tom was 69 when he came to see a counsellor; he had lost his wife two years earlier.

Tom: I've read the books about this gestalt. And I've read about bereavement. I should have got over it by now, I know.

Th.: What's this 'it'?

Tom: O, you know. The bereavement.

Th.: That's the loss of someone you love. I don't know your wife's name.

Tom: [begins to weep quietly] What I've got to face is that it's all over.

Th.: Again that word 'it'.

Tom: [After a pause, stands] I said face it. Got to do that sooner or later. Better be now with someone there. You're all right, are you? [The therapist nods quietly. Tom stands and faces the wall, and mops his eyes.] I'm facing it. No, you said not 'it'. [After a long pause he speaks again] Sarah. [He bends over, convulsed with sobs, then turns to the therapist] I knew I had to say it, it's so stupid.

Th.: See if there's more to say to Sarah now, if you face around again.

Tom found more and more to say, some of it not comprehensible to the therapist, but all seeming part of a painful farewell and thanks to a woman to whom he had been devoted and who he had always supposed would live longer than he. When he had finished, he said how he had suddenly realised when the therapist commented 'it' that he kept at bay the reality of his wife's dying, by avoiding her name and his memory of her, even sleeping in the spare room since she died.

This intelligent man had in a first session invented his own experiment, and then made sense of it, made a conclusion or learning.

Many people equate gestalt therapy with two-chair work. Perhaps as a result, the technique is less taught and used in many institutions than in the middle of the last century. As a further result, it can happen that two-chair experiments are undertaken without being carried through to the most useful place.

Here then is an extensive example of such an experiment. It took place later in the session with Gwen.

Gwen: Now I feel that you are not really interested in me at all. [The therapist is tempted to protest that she is seemingly more interested in the client than the client is with her. She realises that this would be like the self-justifying statements the client complains that her mother makes. She notices her own defensive irritation, and remembers that the client has already spoken of the irritation that she has shown in many ways since she came in. There is a pause.]

Th.:   If we imagine me sitting on that empty chair, you could say whatever you need to, to that pretend me.

Gwen: If I felt like it.

Th.:   Yes, only if you feel like it. [The therapist imagines the conflict between the client's pattern of blaming and being aggrieved, on the one hand, and on the other, wanting to co-operate, discover more of herself, and be happier. This side seems uppermost. Gwen turns to a third chair making a triangle between them, and speaks to it.]

Gwen: You didn't even see me right to the door last week, just because your phone went. Well I can't bear you having all the answers and knowing better than I do. And everything tidy and I don't ask you to clear up after me. It gets on my nerves. All right,

I know you sent me to good schools. [She breaks off and turns to the therapist] I've turned you into my mother.

Th.: You've stopped. Or you could go on. Would you like to experiment more, with me directing?

Gwen: Yep.

Th.: Sit in that chair and speak as her. [Gwen moves across] Give yourself a moment to find how to be her. How she holds her head. How she looks at you. How... [Gwen looks pinched and disapproving and speaks in a thin voice]

Gwen: After all your father did for you. He wanted you to be a doctor, and do something with your life, instead of trailing round with that dreadful man. I told you he'd leave you and he did. And you waste your talent in that shop.

Th.: Change places, and respond to what she's said. [The therapist is now behaving as director of the experiment, making clear suggestions that she hopes will advance the work.]

Gwen: [From her own place, to the mother-chair. Her voice is subdued] I hate you for saying that. Because I agree. I'm 26 and I'm nowhere, and I'm stuck at home because the rents are so ghastly in London.

Th.: You say you hate her for saying that.

Gwen: Well in reality she doesn't say any of it, but she must think it.

Th.: So you're saying aloud things you think about yourself. And it's just a guess that your mother thinks the same. Sit in her chair again. [After moving across slowly, Gwen is silent] I don't know if you are imagining your mother being silent, or if you are holding something back.

Gwen: I'm holding back. I don't want to let her...

Th.: [Interrupting] Now you're speaking as yourself, so move back to your chair, to keep matters clear for yourself. [Gwen moves] You said 'I don't want to let you...'

Gwen: [With effort] I don't want to let you... I don't want to let in that you really are worried about me. I can't bear it, it's so painful.

Th.: See if you find the words to tell her some of that pain.

Gwen: [Crying] She does her best not to let me see that she's worried stiff about me.

Th.: You. You do your best not to let me see.

Gwen: I can't. It's worse to say it to her right out.

Th.: You can do it, Gwen. If you want to. [Pause]

Gwen: It's like I'm going dizzy, all the edges going.

Th.: [Softly, after a pause] What does she do her best to keep you from seeing? Tell her.

Gwen: [To the empty chair, speaking breathlessly and disjointedly] I know Aunt Beth wants you to move to Kent and live with her, and you want to. But you stay in London for me. And you don't nag me to go back to college. And we both know I'll get nowhere without a degree.

Th.: Tell her the feeling you have towards her as you say that.

Gwen: [Sobbing] I love you.

Th.: And now move to her place. [Gwen moves] Find what your mother wants to say to you.

Gwen: I love you. [After some moments she turns to the therapist] It's so ridiculous. I know she loves me but I hadn't realised how I sort of kept it out. And of course I love her, I'd say so to anyone, but I've been keeping that out. I'd made her into my conscience, the part of me that says all that about degrees and stuff, that I've been stuffing my ears not to hear. Whew.

This is an account of a very intense piece of two-chair work, quoted here partly because it was comparatively brief, as well as showing many of the features of an experiment that led to obvious change. It is also an example of Beisser's paradoxical theory of change. This involves acceptance of a present reality, often one that has – like this one – been suppressed or denied, as Gwen herself comments at the end of the work. Beisser suggested that the acceptance itself brings about change, as has happened here. Gwen has let in, emotionally accepted, what lay under the conflict that brought her to the consulting room. Gwen also experienced another phenomenon noticed in this theory. She went into an impasse, an almost fugue or panic state she described as going dizzy, with all the edges going, as she let go of her present story of herself and accepted what was her real truth. An important footnote is that in time the counsellor recalled Gwen's annoyance with her, and they resolved the real slight the therapist had inadvertently given. Two-chair work is not an avoidance of confrontation but a means of exploring the projective elements in it.

Perls once said something to the effect that the client's job is to evade the present, and the therapist's job to work relentlessly to keep him in the present. You will see how in this piece of work the therapist worked towards that. She re-phrased what Gwen said, when she used the third person, rather than staying in direct dialogue. She also paid close attention to what Gwen was saying and how she was saying it, and did not let her continue speaking from one chair, when her words meant she had switched roles. Part of the task was to unplait or unknot the snarl of messages inside Gwen, and let her see where she attributed them. Separation of elements was needed before a new integration could happen.

At its simplest it seems as if Gwen had sunk under the weight of expectations from her father and implicitly from her mother, to the point of refusing to do what she herself wanted to do, just because they wanted it so much. Dr Spock, in his manual for bringing up children, jokingly suggested that spinach should be withheld from them until they had eaten up their pudding. He was commenting on the same phenomenon: other people's hopes and ambitions for you can have a reverse effect, and put you off, make you dislike what you might otherwise enjoy.

Many of us express conflicts as two opposing forces. My head says one thing, my heart another, for example. Putting the two sides of the conflict on two chairs, and shuttling between them, will generally serve to show the energy or force with which they are experienced. This may be the outcome. If the client is willing, the dialogue between the two sides can develop beyond an argument or expression of fear or dislike. The client can come to see the usefulness of each side to the other.

Rita, a widowed mother of two teenage boys, was in therapy in the hope, in her words, of being a better mother. This vignette is the later part of an experiment in which she had named one chair her patience and the other her witch.

Rita: [as Witch, to Patience] You're not patient. You're scared, a fraidy cat.

Th.:   So how can you help her not be a fraidy cat?

Rita: Just stand up to them. [Aside] This is no good. All I can do over here is bully. [changes chairs and speaks as Patience] It's true I'm scared. They're big boys and there's so much trouble they could get into. I need your guts to be firm with them.

Th.:   See what happens to the witch when you tell her that.

Rita: She's stopped looking as if she'll fly off the handle like I said I did on Sunday.

Th.:   Move back there and see what she has to say to Patience.

Rita: [from Witch chair, to Patience] I feel scared of the boys too. And for them. I think we're both important. If we both let go of being so frightened.

Behaviour that Rita had introjected from a meek mother and a stern father was now assimilated into a parenting style that she and her sons could respect and enjoy.

Some of the experiments quoted so far in this chapter have moved along in ways the therapist might have guessed. But the client may change the subject at any moment, or stop dead, or make objections. If the therapist then becomes disconcerted, or determined to push on with what she has started, she may be overlooking some of the evidence in the room. She needs to reflect on how the client stopped what the therapist had perhaps started, whether she and the client are in a power struggle.

Whatever happens when an experiment is begun is an outcome, and learning can be drawn from it. Hugh, a 35-year-old motor mechanic, had been seeing a therapist for several months, to decide whether to tell his wife he was a cross-dresser, and risk losing her and their young son. In supervision, the therapist described how in experiments he would suddenly go into a fugue state, blanking completely.

Supervisor: And what do you do then?

Th.: Well, I sometimes remind him of where we had got to.

Supervisor: That sounds more like steering him on to your path than following his.

Th.: What you're reminding me to do is, in the old phrase, to analyse the resistance. Thanks. I'll try.

In their next therapy session Hugh, at his own request, imagined himself into the scene where he would tell Tracy. He set a chair to represent her, sat and faced it. After a moment he turned to the therapist and said: 'It's no good. It doesn't work.' Her heart sank for a moment, at this familiar stuck place. Then she remembered her supervision.

Th.: So you are telling Tracy it is no good and doesn't work? What is 'it' here?

Hugh: No, I was talking to you, not her. [The therapist remains quiet for what seems a long time] It's ridiculous to start saying the whole marriage doesn't work just because... [There is another pause]

Th.: You didn't finish what you were saying, Hugh.

Hugh: I've forgotten. I'm so stupid.

Th.: What you keep showing me, Hugh, is a sort of pattern. I imagine you get right up close to something that scares you mightily, then a fuse goes, and there's all darkness.

Hugh: That's exactly how it feels.

Th.: And I'm remembering you telling me how secret you have been for so long about the cross-dressing.

Hugh: Always keeping mum. I've made a circuit-breaker that's a bit too bloody sensitive, haven't I?

In time Hugh began to perceive his internal blanks as an impasse that had the potential for a breakthrough, a new discovery.

In terms of what we are looking at here, the therapist had learned that there is always a discovery to be made from any experiment, more especially if the parties to it have not decided beforehand where it should lead or how it should end.

Rehearsal

Some of the experiments described here have led to change via Beisser's paradoxical theory. It is not the only kind of change acknowledged in gestalt therapy. Another is by deliberate learning, often of a social skill missing from a client's repertoire. Robert was a shy young man, most at home working at his computer. In therapy he began to overcome some of the fear of social contact that he had learned from his agoraphobic mother, his sole parent. But one difficulty remained.

Robert: It happened again last night. I hardly ever buy a round of drinks, because I just can't face going up to the bar and insisting on being served. At the thought of it I go right back into all the neurotic tripe I thought I'd left behind. People are starting to snigger about me being mean.

Th.: So you call your terror 'neurotic tripe'?

Robert: Point taken. I mean I know why, I know the back story. I'm just stuck at changing one bit of behaviour.

Th.: Shall we try an experiment?

Robert: Anything.

Th.: Who do you know who always gets himself or herself served?

Robert: O, Jim. He's quite small, but..

Th.: Shut your eyes and imagine him getting a round, and report aloud what you see.

Robert:	[Laughs and opens his eyes] I couldn't do that. I just couldn't. He shouts 'oi' and waves his money in the air. Then he says he'll run between everyone's legs to get to the front, and they laugh and let him through. Well I'm 6 feet tall.
Th.:	You gave me a very clear picture of what he does. So you can't run between people's legs.
Robert:	Just the thought of shouting and waving my money in the air...
Th.:	Show me. We can imagine the bar along that wall. [Robert stands and holds a banknote above his head.]
Robert:	Excuse me.
Th.:	Can anyone hear you?
Robert:	[Takes an uncertain step forward] Please.
Th.:	Use Jim as a model.
Robert:	But I told you...
Th.:	For the parts you can copy.
Robert:	[Clears throat] Oi.
Th.:	Once more with feeling.
Robert:	Oi! [He looks at the therapist and grins] Well that didn't hurt. Only there's no-one there. It's the crowd that scares me.

For the following session Robert met the therapist at a busy nearby pub.

Robert:	My impulse was to find a table up in that corner, but I've stayed standing here in this throng. So I'm winning.
Th.:	I'd like a drink.

Robert succeeded in getting the barmaid's attention, and felt ready to do so again with his friends. Laura Perls once said that every new patient requires a new therapy. In gestalt therapy, the inventiveness of client and therapist may usefully, if rarely, take them outside the regular time and place of meeting, when that seems needed.

Dreams

Whatever occurs in a dream is part of the dreamer, at least in the sense that it is the dreamer's memory or re-working or imagining that is the dream. Gestalt therapy extends this reality in one way it offers of working therapeutically with dreams. The projective part of every element of the dream is explored, as this brief example describes. Sue, a married career woman of 34, had been in therapy for some months, working on whether to take a job in Geneva and only see her husband at weekends, or insist on his following her there.

Sue: There's this half-memory in my mind, or p'raps it was a half-dream. But it won't go away. I just get into this first-class railway carriage and settle down, only... [She pauses]

Th.:   So are you giving me half a dream now?

Sue: Sorry. I was trying to work out what wasn't there. Something forgotten. I'd really like to work on it today.

Th.:   Then shut your eyes and go back into the dream, and tell it again in the present tense.

Sue: [After a moment] I'm remembering...

Th.:   Stay in the present.

Sue: I've just got a seat and I'm pleased. Though there's no-one else there. I put my bag down and hear the carriage door clunk behind me and now the train's moving and I stand up. I'm suddenly really worried. [She stops and opens her eyes] That's all there is. But it's so vivid.

Th.:   Imagine yourself as that carriage door. What are you like?

Sue: I'm very strong. Clunk. I won't open once the train's moving. I'm security.

Th.:   So what are you saying to Sue, door?

Sue: You're safe with me. You won't fall out. [To the therapist] It's Geneva: first-class cushy job, guaranteed security. But a bit final.

Th.: Just for now let's delay talking about, and explore more if you're willing. If you're ready to, imagine yourself as the missing part of the dream.

Sue: [After a pause] This is difficult. Well, I'm outside the train, that's for sure. And Sue can't see me. But she's searching. I think I'm the other case she left behind. [Sue looks startled] The other case. The other case I've never talked about to you, even though you've raised it. The other case is staying at home and having a family.

In the following weeks Sue discovered that she was just pregnant when she had the dream. She saw the train as representing either the security of the new job, or the inexorable progress of what became a very welcome pregnancy.

The assumption, in this way of working with dreams, is that the more inanimate any element of the dream is, the more the dreamer has disguised its significance. So the therapist tends to begin the various identifications there. In supervision this therapist criticised herself for not beginning with the missing part of the dream, which was certainly the most disguised. Her supervisor said that all roads lead to Rome, and the therapist and Sue had learned enough from exploring just two elements, no matter in what order.

This way of working on dreams is often very productive. It deals with the projective aspect of dreaming. Sometimes, as in any work with a client's projections, more work is then needed on relationship. A client dreamed of her therapist as a torturer who tied her to a chair and stuck a knife in her. They did much work on the client's maternal projections, boss projections, and tendency to hostility. Then the therapist said she remembered her own moment of anger the week before, and what she called a waspish intervention she had made, and for which she apologised. She and the client came through this to a better trust of each other.

As these examples show, experiments are almost always in the service of relationship, making contact more full and rewarding for both people.

Sigmund Freud expressed the very same idea:

> In the individual's mental life someone else is invariably involved, as a model, as an object, as a helper, as an opponent, and so from the very first individual psychology ... is at the same time social psychology as well. (Freud 1921:83)

Experiment

Sculpt

If you are with other people, focus on a fragment of conversation between two of them. Ask them to stand, and then sculpt, or move them into positions which to you convey the attitudes they had to each other in their verbal exchange. If you are alone, you may recall some lively exchange you have witnessed, and imagine again the sculpt of the two speakers. If you are working with people in the room, let them in turn sculpt their perception of the conversation.

SIX

Integration and Evolution of Gestalt

Gestalt therapy itself represents an integration of many sources of inspiration to the founders. Heraclitus' observations, gestalt psychology, Freud's theories, existentialism, Lewin's field theory, Reich's character armour (1972), Taoism and Moreno's social experimentation among others, have contributed some of the parts that have been organised into the whole we call gestalt therapy. None of them have been swallowed whole. These sources exist in a partial, assimilated form here. It is in line with Perls' analogy of eating with the taking in of experience, that as time goes by, new ideas and methods are integrated into the original theory, and so it grows and changes. This is a catholic method:

> it is absurd to think even for a moment of not combating the resistances, of not rousing anxiety, of not showing that a neurotic response does not work, of not reviving the past, of witholding all interpretation and discarding one's science ... what is the reality of an interview in which one of the partners, the therapist, inhibits his best power, what he knows and therefore evaluates? (PHG 1951: 286)

In the training of this discipline, there is often and understandably an insistence on staying with the methods and assumptions of the original writers. As in other schools, the interpretation of these varies between establishments and practitioners. Attention to physical behaviour, strict accurate language, true phenomenological dialogue, even experiment are variously insisted on or left out by trainers and therapists who see themselves as pure gestaltists.

Heraclitus was the first philosopher we know to have recorded that all is dynamic, all is constant change. This chapter will emphasise that gestalt is not a competitive pitch for one philosophy and method, but at best a demonstration of respectful and useful embracing and adaptation of ancient and new ideas and methods. Yontef (1993) states that gestalt may use any techniques as long as they are aimed at increasing awareness, arise from phenomenological dialogue, and are within the parameters of ethical conduct. This in line with Laura Perls' dictum often quoted in this book, that every new client requires a new therapy.

There is a general movement in psychotherapy towards integration of different theories and methods. One outcome of this is that various forms of experiment have been adopted from gestalt into other therapies. There are many fewer methods or techniques in other therapies that are not already available to this one. What is more, Perls was, from the first, eager that therapists should use what he called their best powers. Always averse to categories, he was sensitive to the difference of style there will always be between different practitioners. The founding pair of gestalt, Fritz and Laura Perls, advocated flexibility and resourcefulness from the therapist. The important concept of humility, staying with not-knowing, of refusing to jump to a prescribed intervention, supports this flexibility. Allowing the novelty of the new present to impact her, the therapist may need to experience a moment of impasse, of blanking, then of waiting for the emergence of her next therapeutic awareness and a novel intervention.

A move towards integration can be seen in many contemporary schools of psychotherapy. From its beginnings, this one has insisted on the value of creativity, on using 'the best powers of the therapist'. In that way it has always been open to subsume the therapeutically effective treatment from any source, as another experiment.

Here we look at some of the newer discoveries and theories that have affected or been adopted in gestalt.

Neuroscience

Neuroscience is perhaps the latest and most exciting set of discoveries in psychology. It has let people see more of how we respond, what actually happens in our bodies in perception. We now can witness, for example, how neural pathways are made and reinforced by repeated actions. This understanding can help therapist and client to be respectful of the effort it can take to create a new pathway, and so change a habit of perception or behaviour.

Neuroscience has largely supported gestalt hypotheses about how we operate. Interestingly, it nevertheless at times shows a difference between belief and actuality. On occasion, for example, action comes before awareness. Reflexes such as recoiling from burning substances are now understood to happen before we register in awareness what the pain and danger were. In this albeit limited way, Zinker's cycle of awareness is further shown to be an invalid descriptor.

In this new science, more discoveries are constantly made, as the technology of brain-scanning improves. These are likely to change our understanding of processes, while not necessarily altering therapeutic practice. One perhaps important instance is quoted here, of a possible biological explanation of some of our social nature, of sympathy and empathy.

Mirror neurons

As far as we can tell, humans are the only species with a greatly developed capacity for imagining, empathising and sympathising with what is going on in another person or creature. Our need for this empathic ability from others sometimes shows in an insistence that a dog or horse or other animal knows just what we are feeling or need. But humans have a massively larger power than other animals to sense the experience of another person. Mirror neurons, accidentally discovered during an experiment, seem to lie adjacent to motor neurons inside us. They fire as we see or even hear what other people are doing, so that we perform an internal, as-if version of what they are experiencing. We do this all day long, often out of awareness. It looks as if this capacity is a great part of our empathic ability, our ability to guess with some accuracy what is going on in someone in feeling terms, as well as in their behaviour. This discovery bears out Perls' observation that intensity of behaviour is an important criterion.

We are social animals, responsive to each other at every level. Except in some pathological states, even avoidance of people is a sign of strong reaction to them, rather than indifference. So, even to the cautious neuroscientists, it is arguable that empathy and social response are not a compromise but a gratification, as this theory believes.

Recently the idea has occurred to neuroscientists that this capacity can also be retroflective. Oberman and Ramachandran (2009) have speculated that mirror neurons may provide the neurological basis of human self-awareness, as well as sensitivity to others. In an essay written for the Edge Foundation in 2009, Ramachandran gave the following explanation of his theory:

> I also speculated that these neurons cannot only help simulate other people's behavior but can be turned 'inward' – as it were – to create second-order representations or meta-representations of your own earlier brain processes. This could be the neural basis of introspection, and of the reciprocity of self awareness and other awareness. There is obviously a chicken-or-egg question here as to which evolved first, but … The main point is that the two co-evolved, mutually enriching each other to create the mature representation of self that characterizes modern humans.

Here is a powerful discovery of one of the biological, observable mechanisms that in earlier times might have been termed intuition or a form of spirituality.

Autonomy and co-creation

Intensity of contact with experience is an internal phenomenon. Gestalt is concerned with allowing the fullness of all experience, the intensity of feeling, sensing and doing, that constitutes a rich way of living. Early theorists stressed this individual responsibility for how we experience. Co-creation of experience has fascinated more recent gestalt theorists: circumstances must influence how we respond. To take dramatic examples of this, if I am in a country where the crops and rains fail, staying alive will likely be my major concern. If I live under a tyrannical regime, I have very different existential choices available, compared with someone who lives in a prosperous democracy. Abraham Maslow's hierarchy of needs was contemporaneous with early gestalt theory. It suggests that until our basic survival needs are taken care of, we do not have much energy for what he termed self-actualisation. We are psychologically as well as materially impoverished. This theory is greatly criticised now as self-centred and down-playing our social nature. There is a thread of truth in it that has perhaps become unfashionable as relational psychotherapy has come strongly into focus in recent times.

Relational gestalt

Maslow's embeddedness in his own individualistic culture has been part of the reason for his ideas and their representation in gestalt theory being strongly criticised. As stated earlier in this book, thinkers belonging to the years soon after the Second World War could not but be influenced by that. Truth is contextual, dependent on its environment, as gestalt insists. The regimentation and need for conformity of the war years produced focus on the nation rather than on oneself. Patient acceptance of conscription to the armed forces, with all the awful consequences of fighting, was widespread. Rationing of food and clothes, obeying directives to spend what might have been leisure as fire-watchers or in other unpaid tasks, conforming to the strictest blackout rules, are examples of the quashing of individual choice at that time. It is in accordance with gestalt theory that a swing to the other pole would result, and it did, though not as thoroughly as is sometimes alleged.

The richness of life is very largely to do with relationship, an idea said to be under-emphasised and often only implicit in early theory. But 'the lapse of community in political societies is not reducible to the neurosis of individuals, who indeed have become "individuals" because of the lapse of society ... it is a disease of the field, and only a kind of group-therapy would help' (PHG 1951: 354). In the same paragraph we read: 'all individual personality and all organised society develop from functions of coherence that are essential to both person and society [love, learning, communication, identification ...]'. The distinction between intrapersonal and interpersonal is stated as less than useful. Organismic self-regulation is seen as, in part, disengaging from more unreliable systems such as money, power, competition and prestige, to re-engage with 'the primary personal systems of love, grief, anger, community, parenthood, dependence and independence' (p. 355). In other words, what is now seen as new, and named relational gestalt, was there from the first. This welcome new emphasis sits alongside the existential aloneness of every human. Contact and withdrawal is the rhythm by which we all live.

Co-creation

It takes two to tango. This idea is implicit in the gestalt concept of contact. It is elaborated usefully by the term co-creation, which is now widely used. The sense of co-creation is exemplified as well in phenomenological dialogue as anywhere. In it, each speaker pays full attention to the effect on him or her of the other, and reports that. Finally, it is individual truth that is being sought. But it is through relationship that that is made possible. The seemingly almost paradoxical ideas of autonomy and indivisibility from the environment are held together here. Long ago Harry Stack Sullivan stated that the self is forged in interaction. This brief statement encapsulates the ideas of co-creation and the loneliness that he was said to know as a child.

De-structuring, breaking down to elements and then forming a new gestalt can be seen in some developments of gestalt. It is a process intrinsic to it, and seems vital in any theory which incorporates environment with the present. What also shows from time to time is the old sport of killing the fathers. Perls himself can be argued to have played this game with vigour, in his 'Revision of Freud's Theory and Method' (1969[1947]). More recently he has been on the receiving end of similar attempts, to the point of the allegation that Goodman wrote the 1951 book. It then begins to sound as if Goodman invented gestalt therapy. But the theory was there in *Ego, Hunger and Aggression,* written by Perls alone five years before. Paul Goodman, who was a large influence on the anti-materialist social culture of young Americans in the 1960s, emphasised the social implications of the theory. Jacob Moreno, whose remarkable inventiveness in social experiments in the 1920s preceded Perls and Goodman, was another large contributor to the social awareness of the original thinkers and to their methods.

Developmental theory

Psychologists have in modern times become more and more sensitive to the apparent effects of early life on every one of us. Present thinking in most therapies is that what happened when and how in childhood has enormous influence on how we live the rest of our lives. Early experience, and our early responses, seem likely to become more embedded in our perceptive capacity than later happenings.

Perls was less interested in the content of early memories than in the fact that 'the childish feeling and attitude that lived that scene are of the utmost importance' (PHG 1951: 297). He in no way discounted the importance of childhood, and wrote passionately of the desirability of recovering what he called the childhood attitude of earnestness, by which he meant full involvement in activity, with clarity about how action and fantasy are combined.

What he omitted was any account of how awareness develops in humans from the day they are born or before. The exception to this is his aetiology of neurosis. He suggested that the progress from being a suckling to being weaned, via the beginning of dentition, is a major clue to how we take in or reject all experience throughout life. This idea is more fully explained in the first chapter of this book.

Daniel Stern's account of child development has since been adopted into gestalt. He appears to think in ways analogous to this theory, not only about infantile perception, but in his study of the nature of the present moment (Stern 2004). Daniel Stern is an American psychiatrist and research psychologist. His intensive studies of early childhood led him to many conclusions that overlap strikingly with gestalt ideas. Many gestalt training institutes now use his description of how we all start off in life. In 1992 the international Association for the Advancement of Gestalt Therapy formally adopted him as a theorist.

In brief, he saw four major stages of infant development. He called the very first months the stage of forming the emergent self. By this he meant what in gestalt might be called the beginning of gestalt formation, the organising of data into recognisable patterns, sequences, meanings. He suggests that the newborn baby is gradually, already, getting together some useful notions. In caricature, one of these might be face-near-me; special smell; warm arms; breast; happy feeling. Later, the word mother will be a cypher for all this and more. So even at the very beginning of life, Stern is one of the growing number of psychologists who are convinced that it is human nature to be in contact and interaction with differentiated others. He calls another characteristic of this phase alert inactivity. The baby is not just lying there, she is noticing and learning. She is creating meaningful units of perception from all the new data crowding in on her. Without thinking about it, many people behave as if they recognise this, as they speak to newborns in a higher voice than usual, probably more softly, and with plenty of smiles and assurances to the little one that she is special, or more likely the very finest of her kind. Many of us recognise the needs of the new little person to be recognised, applauded and welcomed into the group.

Another important aspect of this early time, and one strongly implicit in gestalt theory, is what Stern calls vitality affects. Affect is psychologese for emotions and feelings. The feelings – joy, anger, sadness and so on – are sometimes called Darwinian, because Charles Darwin wrote a whole book describing them (Darwin 1990). But Stern also noticed the importance of the intensity, the pace, cadence and rhythm of any experience, and called that the vitality affect. Babies use their whole bodies to express themselves. You have seen an infant, faced with a favourite toy, not just smiling and reaching towards it but kicking and arching. It is the how of showing feeling that Stern calls the vitality affect. The subtitle of the original book, *Gestalt Therapy*, was *Excitement and Growth in the Human Personality*. Excitement is a vitality affect. Like the rest of this emergent phase, it does not go away, but in Stern's view is re-experienced in all creative acts throughout life. Creativity involves uncertainty and making something out of a new, perhaps still rather vague or confused, field of data.

From two months on, this tendency to organise and create order becomes stronger, and it looks as if the new person is making a coherent sense of herself. Stern calls this the core self. It consists of a sense of self-agency, an awareness of being able to do things, like deliberately looking or fussing or smiling, and getting particular responses from the carers. With this comes noticing self-coherence, knowing for instance that discomfort and crying hang together, that sucking hard and then feeling sleepy and contented are a complete cycle, or what in this theory would be termed a complete gestalt.

Alongside these observations, often repeated, comes a sense of self-history. These things have often happened. So I know how to do them. Rather than still being at that early stage of having to learn from nowhere, as the creative emergent self, now there is a repertoire of learned interactions with things and people. Stern calls these repeated interactions that are generalised, RIGs for short. They are fixed gestalts, ways of doing things that have been learned and can be repeated without much creative effort. We all function on a huge repertoire of RIGs. Some, like how to greet different people, stay mostly in awareness. Many, perhaps like driving a car, are partly out of awareness. I say this from the experience of helping someone learn to drive, and realising that I did better by describing the actions of eye, foot, or hand, as I did them, than theorise about them when not in the car.

From seven months or some weeks later, the baby has worked enough at all this ordering and organising inside herself, to give even more attention to how she gets on with other people. Intersubjectivity becomes the work. She has been doing some of this since day one of her life. But now there seems to be much more interest in the feelings of other people. Empathy, the quality that allows us to feel for and guess at the feelings of others, comes to the fore. She experiments with the power of evoking responses in others, and sees her mother or sibling or father smile back when she smiles, or pull a sad face when she is grumpy. This is clearly a shared world, and one in which she can both evoke responses and attune her feelings to other people.

From now on, she also takes in the capacity to change modalities, to make a tune into a body movement, say, by beating time. Or the carer will lift her high in the air and make a rising sound, wheeee. Then the baby will say wheeee as a request for another lift. Symbolism, having one thing stand for another, is coming clearer in this sophisticated little mind. Playing, holding an awareness of what is, and what is pretend or as-if, advances. Teddy is made to drive a train; she can pull a cover over herself and have people call out that she has disappeared. What power!

As she begins moving about and then walking, she gets more and more adept as an imitator. Aristotle described imitation as the earliest form of learning, and the neuroscientists seem to agree with him. Most carers are eager to have babies imitate sounds and syllables, and babies usually behave as if they feel the same. Intentions and meanings are being more and more shared between the baby and those around her. So by the age of 18 months that most remarkable symbolic system, human language, is being tackled in earnest.

Until then, experience is irrefutable. What is felt is felt. What happens happens. Then, as language is acquired, it becomes possible to elaborate, to share nuances of feeling, to understand what it is that made Daddy late or the dinner burnt. The narrative self has emerged. And for perhaps the first time it also becomes possible to falsify. When a cross person asks who spilt the juice, fear and creativity may help the culprit say it was the cat, or a brother, who did it. With the advent of language, a split in the sense of self perhaps becomes possible, according to Stern.

Attachment theory

A British researcher, John Bowlby (1999), gave weight to different observations in his work with mothers and babies. Working some time back in the last century, his ideas were, like everyone's always, constrained by context, by what he took for granted in the society round him. What he knew were families where generally the father went to work, and the mother stayed home and looked after the children. He saw that first pair, the mother and child, as massively important in the child's development of relationship throughout her life. He saw the baby needing closeness, gentleness, feeding, which would become part of her own ability to love and to trust. Like Perls, he saw contact as a central need. What the baby learned in this first pair, he suggested, would influence all her relationships in later life. This idea overlaps with Stern's repeated interactions that are generalised, RIGs. It has echoes of what Perls called a fixed gestalt, an idea that is projected over and over again. Later researchers, notably Judy Dunn (1993), have stressed the impact of other early relationships, with father, siblings and other children. But the core of Bowlby's observations remains of great use in observing present behaviour.

Perls saw curiosity and excitement as major tools of fulfilled living. Bowlby, watching mothers and infants together, noticed how some babies would crawl or totter away from the mother, look to see that she was there, and soon return. Gradually they would venture away for longer and longer intervals, and become interested in toys or activities or other people. He called this secure attachment, as a way of describing the baby's trust that she could venture away and still be accepted back with the mother or carer. This trust, he saw, was not simply a decision of the baby's but came about because many previous interactions of the pair had reassured the baby of the mother's reliability. The style of attachment is co-created, fashioned from both sides. It makes for experienced, adventurous babies, who have tried out falling and being pushed over and licking coal and myriad other strange and informative experiences, by a very young age.

According to their behaviour, and the different temperaments of the mothers and babies, other styles of attachment form. Anxious attachment comes about when the baby seems not to want to leave the mother, but needs constant reassurance that the mother is there or happy or at least not sad. Other babies develop avoidant attachment. They are massively aware of the mother, but refuse much interaction with her, either from a need to punish her or to keep out of possible harm's way. They seem wary and a bit lonely, with a distrust that may colour most of their later contacts and prevent stable relationship.

Group therapy

The early gestalt practitioners used groups for training, but the training was in individual therapy. The dynamics of the training group itself were not made a topic of learning. Then gestalt therapy groups came in, but again were largely used as arenas for one-to-one encounters, often between the facilitator or leader and one participant at a time. Many such groups still happen. They have their own usefulness, part of it being the chance for many people to learn the style and skills of the perhaps well-known leader.

Influenced by Freudian and Kleinian group training, and by the group work of Carl Rogers (Kirschenbaum and Henderson 1990), gestalt group therapy has now also become a discipline which deals with the complexities of the interaction of all the participants. The different responses of each to other, the currents of competitive and co-operative feelings which happen far more obviously in a group than in a one-to-one encounter, then become the basis of awareness-raising, dialogue and experiment. Developmental processes happen in groups as well as persons, often in an analogous way. Stern's infant observations are often seen to throw light on the way a group develops or tends to stick at a stage. The out-of-awareness processes described by Bion (1961), and the undeviating trust of Rogers (1961) in the will in the group to achieve appropriate organisation, are two of the many influences which inform modern gestalt group theory (Houston 2003). Gestalt is perhaps the first discipline to integrate two such apparently opposing sets of ideas as these two writers might seem to argue. Their underlying likeness is in an often unacknowledged way the underpinning of much useful gestalt small group work, as well as underpinning gestalt organisational and systems intervention. This often prophylactic use of gestalt therapy theory is arguably its strongest potential.

Pathological processes

The early gestaltists avoided categorisation of their clients, seeing this as dehumanising and leading to treatment of symptoms rather than persons.

In the 1960s there was a tendency to blame society for labelling people as sick, rather than admit the sickness in society. Accurate as this might have been, it sometimes led to a denial of mental illness. Welcome remains of this attitude persist, as in Phillippson's insistence on describing people's contact styles, rather than the more judgemental 'interruptions to contact' (2009). Alongside this Delisle (1999) has described what he freely names as personality disorders, with a respectful indication of the continuum between what is seen as healthy and what is dysfunctional. To all this he adds recommendations of how to diagnose and respond in gestalt methodology.

Integration

A male lawyer came to therapy, wanting to feel and behave better towards his wife of two years. In an early session this intellectual man said: 'Part of the problem is Ann's mother. She is unbearable, and a complete contrast to mine.' The therapist reported in supervision that she had been astonished to hear herself respond: 'I think Melanie Klein would have understood that.' To her supervisor she added: 'Such a heady remark! I thought I'd left that training behind me. Maybe I was competing with him.'

'Or maybe', said the supervisor, 'you were contacting him where he could best hear you. What happened then?' The therapist admitted that the lawyer had eagerly accepted the idea of good breast and bad breast, and himself suggested how he wanted his wife to be his mother in many respects. With that client and that therapist at that time, it seemed that referring to Melanie Klein, rather than exploring the same material through the gestalt method of looking at polarities, made for fruitful dialogue.

Another gestalt therapist, who had first trained in psychodynamic methods, worked with Grace, an 18-year-old who came for help to overcome her intense anger with her parents. She gave many examples of what she called her mother's irrationality and callousness, including allowing dahlias in the garden, though, unbeknown to the mother, Grace disliked them. The therapist felt puzzled to the point of being lost. She stayed with this discomfort, wondering what she was missing. Then she remembered the idea of searching for the significant missing element. She realised that for her it was the father. Grace shrugged and dismissed him. The therapist suddenly felt that the Oedipal triangle, Freud's concept, was worth exploring. Grace was willing to take part in an experiment with three sea-shells that lay on a side table. Using them to represent the three people in her family, they began what became a long journey to uncover Grace's true feelings about each parent and about herself. A Freudian idea had been adapted to good effect into gestalt methodology. The therapist had used her best powers, rather than trying to screen off old knowledge.

Difference

It is not always remembered that Freud said that all psychotherapy is sociotherapy. Gestalt is a reminder to keep awareness of the social nature of human change and integration. It is sometimes difficult for the natives of a country to remember the indivisibility of self and environment, of self and other, when confronted by people who look different and behave differently from them. What Stern would call old RIGs, repeated interactions that have been generalised, suddenly do not operate. A person laughs, but turns out to be embarrassed rather than amused. Someone refuses to meet your eyes but will be found, if enquiry is made, to be showing respect rather than being shifty.

Careful phenomenological dialogue is an excellent route to discovering what is going on for client and therapist from different cultures. Without this, it is easy for the **contact-boundary** to harden into fear, bewilderment and mutual distrust. Just as denial about parts of the self is a usually inadequate way of coping, so denial or exclusion of the changing social environment created by other races, cultures and belief systems is finally a kind of self-denial.

Shame, guilt and fashions in neurosis

Neurasthenia is a term rarely used now, but it was current even in the 1950s. Hysteria was a major topic for Freud, but that again is not at the forefront of most psychological studies. Anorexia nervosa was hardly known outside the medical profession until 1978, when Hilde Bruch published *The Golden Cage: The Enigma of Anorexia Nervosa*. In other words, there seems to be a spirit of the times which prompts us to show un-ease in different forms at different times. This may be strongly allied to suggestions from current publicity and from professionals.

In our times, shame has been a focus for many gestaltists. Alice Miller claims that 'many people suffer all their lives from this oppressive feeling of guilt, the sense of not having lived up to their parents' expectations ... stronger than any intellectual insight, no argument can overcome these guilt feelings, for they have their beginnings in life's earliest period, and from that they derive their intensity and obduracy' (1995: 99–100). In gestalt therapy guilt is used in the dictionary sense, to describe a feeling of wrongdoing, of having committed a bad act. What she names as guilt is generally referred to in gestalt as shame, and is concerned with a feeling of worthlessness. Yontef (1993: 489–523) gives one of the first and most extensive descriptions of what he sees as this common and often overlooked background phenom-enon in therapy. He suggests that it may on occasion be appropriate to feel either guilt or shame, while emphasising the delicacy needed in detecting and responding to it therapeutically. He points out that the polarity of shame is pride, and that this can be a healthy or a distorted response. This is in line with William Blake's dictum from two centuries ago, that 'Pryde is shame's cloke'.

Summary

This concluding chapter serves in part to reinforce the gestalt notion of integrity. By this is meant that the holism of the human organism, our indivisibility from what is around us, is allied with the fact of self-responsibility. We are of the earth. We are such stuff as stars are made of, we are perhaps the quintessence of dust. We are also responsible for our choices, and for evolving ourselves into what we are now. Part of this evolution for any therapist is to integrate her life experience and continuing education, as well as formal training, into her practice. Discoveries about human functioning, and new theories about us, meet the **contact-boundary** and are assimilated into current thinking and practice. Perls said of the major psychotherapy theories, 'all are right, but some are righteous'. This chapter describes some of the ways in which this therapy, like others, is changing emphasis and gathering knowledge as more is learned in many fields. Then the question 'Is this really gestalt?' is sometimes less useful than 'Does this work for this person at this time?'

Glossary

Aggression In gestalt therapy theory, the word is used in its root Latin sense, to mean all outwardly directed activity. In everyday language it more often means hostile activity.

Confluence Flowing together, with loss of boundary clarity.

Contact-boundary Perls and Goodman were fascinated with the mutually constructed boundary between self and other, or, as they termed it, organism and environment. To them, this was the locus of awareness and experience.

Egotism The tendency to be self-observing rather than fully present.

Field A dynamic play of forces that forms a whole, perceived as a shifting figure against a background.

Formation, gestalt This is the configuring or organising process of moving from some disequilibrium or need, through to taking action, and then withdrawing either into gratification or the learning that the action did not achieve what was needed. The four stages of successful gestalt formation are:

> **Fore-contact** The state of quest, unease, disequilibrium which leads to the emergence of a clear figure against a background. A hopeful shopper's discovery of 'Help, I forgot my purse' is a simple example.
>
> **Contact** Following this inner realisation, some action in the world follows. Run home? Borrow from a friend? Explain to the shopkeeper?

Final contact   This in the probably brief moment of sensing 'I did it!' as the friend or shopkeeper smiles, or you get home and find your purse. Money is in your hand again.

Post-contact   Now there is an unwinding. Whew! The relief or gratification of what you have done. The there can be learning: 'I won't go out again without checking my pockets.' And the whole episode starts to fade down and lose interest. You are on an even keel again until the next figure surges into awareness.

Gestalt   The German word is used because there is no exact equivalent in English. It means pattern, or organisation into a form or pattern. The underlying idea is that we all constantly organise fields of data into patterns with transient figures against a particular background.

Introjection   Swallowing whole of what is presented, the way an infant swallows milk. That is a useful introjection. Swallowing whole the idea that other people always know best, or that dancing is the work of the devil, can be worth re-considering and chewing through.

Proflection   Doing to someone else what you would like done to you. Many of us in the caring professions are doing this at least some of the time.

Projection   A cinema projector throws an image forward on to a screen. Seeing something only in another person when it is also part of you is projection.

Retroflection   This word covers two ideas. Literally it means turning back, as when a self-harmer turns anger on himself rather than attacking another person. It is also used to mean what has come to be called proflection.

References

Beisser, A. (1970) 'The paradoxical theory of change', in J. Fagan and I. Shepherd (eds), *Gestalt Therapy Now*. Palo Alto, CA: Science and Behaviour Books.

Bion, W. (1961) *Experiences in Groups*. London: Tavistock.

Bowlby, J. (1999) *Attachment*. New York: Basic Books.

Bruch, H. (1978) *The Golden Cage: The Enigma of Anorexia Nervosa*. Cambridge, MA: Harvard University Press.

Buber, M. (1970 [1922]) *I and Thou*. New York: Scriveners.

Crocker, S.F. (1981) 'Proflection', *The Gestalt Journal*, 4(2).

Darwin, C. (1990) *The Expression of the Emotions in Man and Animals*. London: Folio Society.

Delisle, G. (1999) *Personality Disorders*. Ottawa: Les Editions du Reflet.

De Waal, E. (2010) *The Hare with Amber Eyes*. London: Chatto and Windus.

Dunn, J. (1993) *Young Children's Close Relationships: Beyond Attachment*. London: Sage.

Ellis, W.D. (ed.) (1938) *A Source Book of Gestalt Psychology*. London: Routledge and Kegan Paul.

Freud, S. (1921) *Group Psychology and the Analysis of the Ego*. Harmondsworth: Penguin.

Frew, J. (1992) 'Three styles of Therapeutic Intervention', lecture at AAGT Conference, Boston.

Ginger, S. (2003) *Gestalt Therapy: The Art of Contact*. Paris: Marabout-EPG.

Goodman, P. (1960) *Growing Up Absurd*. New York: Random House.

Houston, G. (2003) *Brief Gestalt Therapy*. London: Sage.

Kierkegaard, S. (2001) *The Kierkegaard Reader*, eds J. Chamberlain and J. Rée. Malden, MA: Blackwell.

Kirschenbaum, H. and Henderson, V.L. (eds) (1990) *The Carl Rogers Reader*. London: Constable.

Lewin, K. (1951) *Field Theory in Social Science*. New York: Harper and Brothers.

Merleau-Ponty, M. (1962) *Phenomenology of Perception*, trans. Colin Smith. London: Routledge and Kegan Paul.

Miller, A. (1995) *The Drama of Being a Child*. London: Virago.

Nevis, S.M. (2003) 'Intimate and strategic behaviour: An integrative perspective', *Gestalt Review*, 7(2).

Oberman, L. and Ramachandran, V.S. (2009) 'Reflections on the mirror neuron system: Their evolutionary functions beyond motor representation', in J.A. Pineda (ed.), *Mirror Neuron Systems: The Role of Mirroring Processes in Social Cognition*. New York: Humana Press, pp. 39–62.

Ovsianka, M. (1928) *Die Wiederaufnahme von unterbrochenen Handlungen Psychologische Forschung*. In: *Psychologische Forschung*.

Perls, F.S. (1969[1947]) *Ego, Hunger and Aggression: A Revision of Freud's Theories*. New York: Random House.

Perls, F.S. (1978) *The Gestalt Approach and Eye-Witness to Therapy*. Palo Alto, CA: Science and Behaviour Books.

Perls, F.S., Hefferline, R. and Goodman, P. (1951) *Gestalt Therapy: Excitement and Growth in the Human Personality*. New York: Dell Publishing.

Phillippson, P. (2009) *The Emergent Self: An Existential-Gestalt Approach*. London: Karnac.

Pursglove, P.D. (ed.) (1968) *Recognitions in Gestalt Therapy*. New York: Funk and Wagnalls.

Ramachandran, V.S. (2009). 'Self awareness: The last frontier', Edge Foundation web essay (1 January): www.edge.org/3rd_culture/rama08/rama08_index.html

Reich, W. (1972) *Character Analysis*, 3rd edn. New York: Simon and Schuster.

Rogers, C. (1961) *On Becoming a Person*. London: Constable.

Sartre, J.-P. (2003) *Being and Nothingness*. London: Routledge.

Stephenson, D.F. (ed.) (1975) *Gestalt Therapy Primer: Introductory Readings in Gestalt Therapy*. Springfield, IL: Charles C. Thomas.

Stern, D. (1985) *The Interpersonal World of the Infant.* New York: Basic Books.

Stern, D. (2004) *The Present Moment.* New York: W.W. Norton.

Stevens, B. (2005) *Don't Push the River.* Highland, NY: Gestalt Journal Press.

Stoehr, T. (1994) *Here Now Next: Paul Goodman and the Origins of Gestalt Therapy.* San Francisco: Jossey-Bass Publishers.

Van Deurzen, E. (2010) *A Handbook of Existential Psychotherapy.* London: Routledge.

Wertheimer, M. (1944) 'Gestalt theory', *Social Research,* 11(1): 78–99.

Yontef, G. (1993) *Awareness, Dialogue and Process: Essays on Gestalt Therapy.* Highland, NY: Gestalt Journal Press.

Zinker, J. (1978) *Creative Process in Gestalt Therapy.* New York: Vintage Books.

Index